HOPI SNAKE CEREMONIES

New Material ©1986 and 2000
Avanyu Publishing, Inc.
P.O. Box 27134
Albuquerque, New Mexico 87125
(505) 341-1280

Original cover art by
Neil David, Sr., Hopi-Tewa

Photography of the cover art by
Focus Advertising, Inc., Albuquerque, NM

Library of Congress Cataloging-in-Publication Data

Fewkes, Jesse Walter, 1850-1930.
    Hopi snake ceremonies.

    Reprint (1st work). Originally published: Tusayan snake
ceremonies. 1st ed. Washington, D.C.: U.S. G.P.O., 1897 in the
Sixteenth Annual report of the Bureau of American Ethnology,
1894 - '95.
    Reprint (2nd work). Originally published: Tusayan flute and
snake ceremonies. 1st ed. Washington, D.C.: U.S. G.P.O., 1900 in the
Nineteenth Annual report of the Bureau of American Ethnology,
1897 - '98.
    Bibliography: p.
    1. Snake-dance. 2. Hopi Indians - Rites and ceremonies.
3. Indians of North America - Arizona - Rites and ceremonies.
I. Title.

E99.H7F329   1986   299'-74   00-110601

ISBN 0-936755-50-4

Back Cover Photo: Hopi Snake Dance, Hopi, Arizona, Courtesy of
The Museum of New Mexico Neg. No. 134951

HOPI SNAKE CEREMONIES

An eyewitness account by
Jesse Walter Fewkes

Selections from Bureau of American Ethnology
Annual Reports Nos. 16 and 19
for the years 1894-95 and 1897-98

Complemented with the addition of selected photographs from the collections of the Museum of New Mexico and the University of New Mexico

Avanyu Publishing Inc.

PUBLISHER'S PREFACE

The Hopi Snake Dance was first described in 1884 and through many articles over the last 100 years has become one of the best known of all aboriginal American Indian ceremonies. Yet, despite its notoriety, it was, and continues to be, little understood by those who are not Hopi Indians. Even so for more than a century, the non-Indian has made the long, and until recently, arduous journey to the Hopis' remote reservation in the Arizona desert. They would come for kachina ceremonies, arts and crafts and contact with the Hopi. They come to watch in amazement as members of the Hopi Snake Society, males of all ages, dance with living rattlesnakes and other venomous reptiles clenched between their teeth. A Hopi has explained the purpose of the Snake ceremonies:

> "They are for the propitiation of the Snake deities and to insure plenty of spring water and abundant rain for the maturing crops. The ceremonies dramatize the legends of the Snake Clan, and the Snake priests gather their 'elder brothers' . . . rattlers, bull snakes and others . . . wash them ritually, and carry them in their teeth during the public dance. They are then released with prayers, to convey to the Rain Deity. Only the pure in mind and heart can dance successfully with the very wise and sacred snake in his teeth."

Sun Chief by Dan Talayesvia, *Arizona Highways*, August 1966.

The most thorough research and first-hand, on-site study ever done on this ceremony was that by noted anthropologist/ethnologist Dr. Jesse Walter Fewkes. Dr. Fewkes (1850-1930) began studying the Snake ceremony in 1891 and continued for six years. His eyewitness accounts are engrossing insights into this ceremony of the Hopi Indians. His writings include all aspects of the lengthy ceremonies: the creation of the altar of the Antelope priesthood; the making of the *pahos* - prayer sticks - by the Antelope priests; the dancing of the Antelope and Snake priests the day before the public plaza dance; the Snake race on the morning of the day of the dance; and, finally the appearance, just before sunset of the Antelope and

Snake priests for the Snake Dance itself. These accounts remain accurate today; the ceremony itself has experienced no appreciable change since Fewkes' time. The Hopi still regularly perform the Snake Dance although not at all five of the villages that Fewkes visited. Since the mid-1980s the Hopi have restricted, and sometimes barred, non-Indians from observing the Snake Dance. Unfortunately the behaviors of some non-Indians at the Dance have denied others from actually experiencing the ceremony.

For those of us who have been fortunate to actually observe the Snake Dance, the experience is more than remarkably memorable. I can remember during a dance watching two of the Hopi participating in the ceremony. One was the dancer, with a three-foot long rattlesnake in his mouth. The dancer was a boy about 11 years old. His companion, the "hugger", was waving two eagle feathers in front of the face of the snake. However, the boy dancer did not have a good grip on the rattler. The snake was wiggling through the boy's teeth until the it had almost circled the boy's neck. The "hugger" finally noticed, and, without an apparent word to the dancer, he grabbed the tail of the snake and pulled it backward through the boy's mouth until the rattler was back in the proper position. The boy's eyes popped wide open with astonishment!

Dr. Fewkes' research was originally published as two papers which were parts of two different Annual reports of the Bureau of American Ethnology. Those were Volume 16 for the years 1894-1895 and Volume 19 for the years 1897-1898. The original pagination of the B.A.E. papers has been retained in this volume. These two articles are brought together here and are supplemented with several photographs from the Photo Archives of the Museum of New Mexico and from the Special Collections Section of Zimmerman Library at the University of New Mexico. Neil David, Sr., eminent Hopi/Tewa artist and kachina doll carver did the splendid original painting on the cover. Look for the two non-Hopis in the painting for the principals of Avanyu.

Avanyu Publishing, Inc.
PO Box 27134
Albuquerque, NM 87125
505 341 1280
email:brentric@aol.com

"PICKING UP THE SNAKES", SNAKE DANCE, HOPI, ARIZONA, 1906, PHOTO BY EDWARD S. CURTIS, COURTESY OF THE MUSEUM OF NEW MEXICO, NEG. NO. 149719

AUDIENCE AT SNAKE DANCE, WALPLI PUEBLO, HOPI, ARIZONA, AUGUST 21, 1913, CA 4:00PM. LARGE MAN IN CAP, LEFT - W.P. HUNT, FIRST STATE GOVERNOR OF ARIZONA, NEXT RIGHT, **IN PITH HELMET - THEODORE ROOSEVELT**, IN FRONT, HEAD TURNED LOOKING UP AT T.R. - SON, KERMIT OR T.R., JR., PHOTO BY H.F. ROBINSON, COURTESY OF THE MUSEUM OF NEW MEXICO, NEG. NO. 37114

HOPI SNAKE DANCE, WALPI PUEBLO, HOPI, ARIZONA, COURTESY OF THE MUSEUM
OF NEW MEXICO, NEG. NO. 166175

SIXTEENTH ANNUAL REPORT

OF THE

BUREAU OF AMERICAN ETHNOLOGY

TO THE

SECRETARY OF THE SMITHSONIAN INSTITUTION

1894-'95

BY

J. W. POWELL

DIRECTOR

WASHINGTON
GOVERNMENT PRINTING OFFICE
1897

TUSAYAN SNAKE CEREMONIES

BY

JESSE WALTER FEWKES

CONTENTS

ILLUSTRATIONS

271

TUSAYAN SNAKE CEREMONIES

By Jesse Walter Fewkes

INTRODUCTORY NOTE

When I began my studies of the Snake dance at Walpi, in 1891, it was said by all the white men whom I consulted that this weird ceremony was confined to the pueblos of Walpi and Micoñinovi, and there was no mention in the literature dealing with the subject of its existence in other villages of Tusayan. During the course of my researches,[1] however, it was discovered that the same or a closely related ceremony takes place in even years at Oraibi and Cuñopavi, and considerable material was collected regarding the exhibition in the latter village in 1892. Shortly after the publication of my memoir[2] on the Snake ceremonials of Walpi, attention was called to the existence of a similar rite in Cipaulovi, so that we are now cognizant of its celebration in five Tusayan villages—Walpi, Micoñinovi, Cuñopavi, Cipaulovi, and Oraibi. As the remaining two pueblos, Sitcomovi and Hano, are now known not to have a Snake dance, we have exact information concerning the Tusayan villages where this ceremony is observed.

The ever-increasing interest in the Snake dance of the Hopi dates from the description by the late Captain J. G. Bourke in 1884. Since the publication of Bourke's valuable book, many articles of more or less scientific value have appeared, so that this rite has now come to be one of the best known of all aboriginal American ceremonials. Most of these accounts, however, deal with the Walpi presentation, and there is a wide field of research still uncultivated in the other pueblos.

The Snake dance at Micoñinovi was first described by Mr Cosmos Mindeleff,[3] and although it has been witnessed by many persons since his article appeared, the ceremony still remains one of the most obscure of all these presentations.

The first notice of the Snake dance at Oraibi we owe to Mr J. H. Politzer, of Phœnix, Arizona, who published numerous newspaper

---

[1] These studies were made in 1896, while the author was connected with the Bureau of American Ethnology.

[2] Journal of American Ethnology and Archæology, Vol. IV.

[3] Science, Vol. VII, June 4, 1886.

accounts of the 1894 presentation, which may be consulted in files of that date. In 1892 Mr R. H. Baxter observed parts of the Cipaulovi or Cuñopavi dances and published a short notice of them in the *American Antiquarian*. It can hardly be said, however, that the accounts by Politzer and Baxter advanced our knowledge of the Snake dance to any considerable degree, as the secret ceremonials were wholly neglected and the public events superficially, often inaccurately, described. They have a value, however, in verifying the statements which had already been made after personal observation of the dances in these three pueblos. Mr Politzer's photographs showed an unexpected fact, that the numbers of participants in the Oraibi dance were small, a feature on which I have elsewhere commented.

From reasons which need not be enumerated, the majority of the descriptions of the Tusayan Snake dance have been limited to the exhibition at Walpi, and our knowledge of this variant far exceeds that of the other pueblos. It is, therefore, but natural that the Walpi dance should be regarded as the most complicated, and while extended research tends to support such a conclusion, it does not necessarily demonstrate that the ceremony at Walpi is the most primitive, but rather tends to show the reverse. To obtain what light we can on this point, as a preliminary to generalizations in regard to the nature and meaning of the Tusayan Snake dance, it is desirable to investigate the details of the presentation in the villages where our knowledge is more fragmentary. The present article is, therefore, offered as a contribution to a study of the Snake dances of Oraibi, Cipaulovi, and Cuñopavi, with generalizations which, it is believed, are warranted by new data obtained from these observations.

The duration of the Snake dance ceremonial at Walpi, where it is celebrated in the most elaborated form, may be stated as twenty days, of which only nine days are marked by active ceremonials, secret or open. Sixteen days before the Snake dance occurs it is formally announced, and on the preceding night the chiefs gather, engage in ceremonial smoking, and commission the town crier to call out the date on the following sunrise.[1] The next seven days are not days of ceremony, although the Antelope chief is engaged in preparations. The eighth day (on which he and others enter the kiva, or "*pakit*," as it is called) is the *yuñya*, or assembly, and for nine days the secret ceremonials continue, closing at sunset of the ninth day by a dance in the plaza, when snakes are carried in the mouths of the participants. The following four days are included in my enumeration, as they are days of purification, but are conspicuous to public eyes only as the frolics, called *nütiwa*, which I have described elsewhere. If these different components are rightly embraced by me in the Snake ceremony, we have, in the twenty days' proceedings, five groups of four days each;

---

[1] The "Oraibi Flute Altar," Journ. Amer. Folk-lore, Vol. VIII, No. xxxi.

The pahoki or shrine in the plaza

The kisi

THE SNAKE DANCE AT CIPAULOVI

W
Y
G
R
B

ALTAR OF THE ANTELOPE PRIESTS AT CIPAULOVI

or, beginning with the last, four days of frolic, four days from the erection of the Snake altar to the Snake dance, four days from the erection
of the Antelope altar to the making of the Snake altar, and eight inact-
ive days, which I am unable to separate by any distinct events.

The nine days of ceremony, beginning with *yūñya* and ending with
the dance, have a nomenclature suggestive of a division into two groups
of four each. The day after the assembly is called the "first day"
(*cüctala*). Then follow the "second day" (*lüctala*), the "third day"
(*paictala*), and the "fourth day" (*naluctala*). The second series then
begins with a second *cüctala*, or "first day," closing with the public
dance.[1] On this basis it will be seen that the number four, so constant
in pueblo ritual, is prominent in the number of days in the Snake ceremonial. I will call attention also to the fact that the nine days of
ceremonies plus the four days of frolic make the mystic number
thirteen. It may likewise be borne in mind that the period of twenty
days, the theoretical length of the most elaborate Tusayan ceremony,
was also characteristic of other more cultured peoples in Mexico, and
that thirteen ceremonials, each twenty days long, make a year of 260
days, a ceremonial epoch of the Maya and related peoples.

The comparative studies which are here considered deal with portions only of the rites of the nine days. This has been necessary on
account of the poverty of data at my control. There seems abundant
evidence that in the three pueblos considered there is no such com-
plexity of secret rites as at Walpi, and consequently there are abbre-
viations. Thus the Antelope altar at Oraibi is not erected on *yūñya*, as
at Walpi, while at Cipaulovi it is made on the second *cüctala*, or only
four days before the dance. When we know all the details of the
Snake ceremonials in each of the five Tusayan pueblos, we shall be able
to draw our comparisons much more closely than at present. This
article, therefore, is preliminary, a temporary summary, or a step, it is
hoped, toward a more exact knowledge of the Snake dances in all the
pueblos of Tusayan.

The dates of the nine days on which ceremonials belonging to the
Snake dances were observed in 1896, at the three villages, are as follows
(the presence of the author is indicated by an asterisk):

	Oraibi	Cipaulovi	Cuñopavi
Yūñya	August 11	August 15*	August 16
Cüctala	August 12	August 16	August 17
Lüctala	August 13	August 17	August 18
Paictala	August 14	August 18	August 19
Naluctala	August 15	August 19	August 20
Cüctala	August 16	August 20	August 21
Komoktotokya	August 17*	August 21*	August 22
Totokya	August 18*	August 22*	August 23
Tihüne	August 19*	August 23*	August 24*

[1] Journ. Amer. Eth. and Archæol., Vol. IV, pp. 13, 14, note.

The secret rites at Cipaulovi took place in the two kivas, the one at the right as one enters the pueblo from Micoñinovi being occupied by the Antelope priests, that on the western side being used by the Snake priests. The Antelope kiva was the same as that occupied by the *Katcina* chief in the *Nimánkatcina,* as I have elsewhere described.[1] The two kivas used at Cuñopavi are at the entrance of the pueblo, that to the left being occupied by the Antelope priests, the one to the right by the Snake priests. The two Oraibi kivas occupied in the Snake dance were on the western side, the one to the right as one emerges from the village being used by the Antelopes, that on the left by the Snake priests,

---

[1] Journ. Amer. Eth. and Archæol., Vol. II, No. I, pp. 99–103.

THE CIPAULOVI SNAKE CEREMONY

GENERAL REMARKS

It has elsewhere been shown that the Snake dance is announced sixteen days before its celebration, after a formal smoke by the chiefs on the preceding night. The nine days of active ceremonials are composed of seven days of secret observances and two of public exhibitions in which dances in the plaza occur. One of these takes place on the eighth day, and has been called the Antelope;[1] the other, on the ninth, is known as the Snake dance proper. The nomenclature of these nine days at Walpi has likewise been given, and the same holds in regard to the days of Snake ceremonials at Cipaulovi, Cuñopavi, and Oraibi. On August 16, the *cüctala*, or first day at Cipaulovi, I visited both Antelope and Snake kivas of this pueblo, but found no altar there. This was exceptional, as compared with Walpi, at the very outset, for in this pueblo the altar is made on the assembly day (*yüñya*). The Antelope chief was present in the kiva, and a bundle of sticks was noticed at the rear end of the room, leaning against the wall. These sticks were the crooks which were later set about the altar in a way which will be described. The chief said the altar would not be made for four days—a statement which I afterward verified—and he added that the Snake dance would occur in eight days. While I was talking with the Antelope chief, the Snake chief came in, and smoked in a formal way; and at the close of the smoke the Antelope chief gave him three strings with red stained feathers tied at their ends (known as *nakwákwocis*), and a small white feather. When the Snake chief received them, he sprinkled a little sacred meal on the bundle of sticks and returned to his own kiva.

So far as I could judge, this ceremony corresponded to the delivery of the prayer-sticks (*pahos*) to Kopeli, the Snake chief, when he went on the snake hunt which I have elsewhere described at length,[2] for the Snake priests immediately set forth on a snake hunt northward from the pueblo. For the next four days this simple ceremony of delivery of the feathered strings to the Snake chief was repeated, and the Snake priests hunted reptiles in the remaining world-quarters, west, south, and east, in the prescribed circuit.

---

[1] The "Oraibi Flute Altar" (see the Bibliography at the close of the article). Strictly speaking, this dance should be called the Corn dance; but as the corn-growing element of the Snake ceremonial is limited to the Antelope priesthood, I retain the name Antelope dance for the public exhibition on the eighth day.

[2] Journ. Amer. Eth. and Archæol., Vol. IV, pp. 40, 41.

There was a small *natci*, made of two sticks tied together, set in the straw matting of each kiva, as at Walpi, and the snake whips of the Snake kiva were arranged upright in a row leaning against the rear wall. This row of snake whips was the only feature comparable with an altar that was constructed in the Snake chamber of Cipaulovi.

As I was obliged to spend the following days at Micoñinovi, studying the Flute observance, no further visits were made to the Cipaulovi kivas until August 21, or the day called *komoktotokya*, when I saw the Antelope altar for the first time, it having been made apparently either that morning or the day before.[1] The Antelope chief, Lomatowa, was absent at the time of my visit, and did not return for several hours, during which I made several visits to the Snake kiva, returning now and then to see the chief when he came back.

THE ANTELOPE ALTAR

The altar of the Antelope priesthood at Cipaulovi (plate LXXI) was the simplest yet reported in any Antelope kiva, but in form and design was closely allied to that at Walpi. The sand picture was large, measuring 4 by 3½ feet, that at Walpi being only about 32 inches square. The kiva was relatively so small, or the sand picture so near the middle of the floor, that one could see it from outside the room by looking through the hatchway. The border, like that of the Walpi altar, was composed of four bands of sand, colored yellow, green, red, and white, respectively, separated by black lines, as in the Antelope sand picture at Walpi. This border inclosed a rectangular field on which were depicted, in different colored sands, the semicircular rainclouds; four yellow, adjacent to the border; three whole and two half semicircles of green; four red, and three whole and two half semicircles in white. All of these were outlined with black lines. On the remaining part of the inclosed rectangle, which was covered with white sand, there were four zigzag figures with triangular heads, one yellow, one green, one red, and one white, beginning at the left of the sand picture as one approached it from the ladder. Each of these figures had a single black mark on the neck representing a necklace, and a curved horn on the left side of the head, and was outlined in black. In the existence of horns on these zigzag figures they differ from the sand picture at Walpi, where two have horns and the other two squares, the former representing males and the latter females. The black dots for eyes were seen in all these symbols of lightning, but the small *nakwákwoci* were not put on their necks, and the annulets and cylinders were not observed on the side of the head, as at Walpi. The row of parallel black lines from the semicircles, representing falling rain, were shorter and more numerous than on the Walpi altar.

At each angle of the sand picture there were conical bodies a few inches high, probably of clay, painted yellow, green, red, and white,

---

[1] *Cüctala*, or "first day" of the second series. It will thus be seen that with the exception of the four snake hunts serious rites were abbreviated in the Antelope kiva.

corresponding with the colors of the cardinal points.[1] At the apices were small feathers.

There were no stone implements on the outer border of the sand picture, as at Walpi, but their places on each side were occupied by a row of clay pedestals, twelve in number on each side, those in each series being placed close together. Each clay pedestal had a straight stick with cornhusk, feather, and string tied to the end. There were none of these sticks at the front of the sand picture, and most of them were not curved at the ends. There were no stone fetishes along the rear of the sand picture, nor stone implements or sticks in pedestals on that side. The *tiponi* was placed back of the extreme right-hand corner, and was separated by a considerable space from the sand picture. Back of the rear edge of the picture, at the right of the median line, there was a small vase and two snake whips standing upright. The floor in front of the picture had about fifteen basket trays, each containing the *pahos* made by individual Antelope priests, and in their midst was the medicine-bowl.

It will be seen that the main points of difference between this altar and that at Walpi are the absence of stone implements, fetishes, and sticks on the front and rear of the picture. The situation of the *tiponi* is different, and there are minor variations in the heads of the lightning symbols and in the arrangement of the sticks and other accessories. The Antelope chief bewailed that his altar was so poor in *wimi* (fetishes), and showed me, in addition to what have been mentioned, a trochid shell and a few rounded stones. I could add to his paraphernalia only a small quartz crystal, which, however, he greatly prized.

The Snake chief at Cipaulovi has no *tiponi*, and consequently no altar. The only objects at the end of the kiva, where the altar would have been had he possessed a *tiponi*, was a row of twenty snake whips leaning against the ledge of the rear wall, behind the *sipapú*. There were two large bags hanging from a peg in the rear wall of the kiva, and on the floor, at one side, four canteens like those which the women use to carry water from the spring to the pueblo. These were full of snakes, and their apertures were stopped with corncobs. The head of an arrowsnake protruded from one of the bags hanging on the wall.

THE CEREMONIES ON THE DAY CALLED TOTOKYA[2]

On August 22, which was the day before the Snake dance at Cipaulovi, I visited both the Antelope and the Snake kiva at about 9 oclock a. m. Both kivas displayed a bow tied across the ladder, about 6 feet above the hatch. These bows had red-stained horsehair hanging to the strings, and a few large feathers suspended at intervals. On the roof, about the hatchway, radiating from the entrance, were six lines

---

[1] The Walpi *Lalakonti* altar has four meal cones in the same positions. American Anthropologist, April, 1892, p. 116, pl. I, fig. 3.

[2] The eighth day of all great ceremonials is called *totokya*. Journ. Amer. Eth. and Archæol, Vol. IV.

of meal on a layer of valley sand, which had been evenly sprinkled on the roof of the kiva. When I entered the Antelope kiva, I found eleven priests assembled there, all engaged in making *pahos* and all with red feathers in their hair. Traces of meal, which had been sprinkled by the priests, were seen on the colored sands of the altar; this was probably an evidence that songs had been sung about it the night before, as I was told had been the case, but was not present.

All the *pahos*, with certain exceptions to be noted, were of the length of the middle finger, and were painted green, with red points. Each *paho* was composed of two sticks, one of which, called the female, had a facet at one end. These *pahos* were tied midway of their length, and to them were attached two herbs, called *kurnyú* and *máabe*. When I called the attention of the priests to the fact that at Walpi *pamnabi* was used instead of *máabe*, they replied that both were equally efficacious, and had the same intent. In addition to the green *pahos*, others, painted black, were similarly employed. The pipe-lighter, who, while not the chief, was most communicative, explained the signification of the offerings he made. They were as follows:

1. A black *paho*.
2. A double-stick green *paho* or *cakwapaho*, with six attached *nakwákwoci*.
3. A green *paho* with green points.
4. A green *paho* with black points.
5. Five white-feathered *nakwákwocis*.

It will be noted that the green *pahos* were of the length of the middle finger, which is very different from the plumed sticks made by the Antelopes at Walpi on the day before the Snake dance, for on that day the Walpians make a *paho* the length of the last two joints of the same finger. On interrogating the priests, I discovered that the Walpi rule was not carried out in Cipaulovi, and that there was no variation in the length of the *paho*.

We have seen how tardy the chief was in making the Antelope altar, and consequently it is apparent why the seven *pahos* of different lengths could not be made, for the sixteen-song celebration was curtailed in the number of presentations, and its equivalent performed only once or twice.

About noon there were brought into the kiva stalks of corn and vines of the bean, cantaloupe, watermelon, and of certain unknown plants. These were done up with yucca thread in two wads or bundles and placed on the altar, after which the man who tied them together smoked on them for some time and then placed the bundles back of the altar. These bundles were carried in the mouth of the participant in the Antelope dance, which, in Cipaulovi as at the other pueblos, occurred at sunset of this day (*totokya*).

At the close of the *paho* making, at about 1.30 p. m., a young man was given a *paho*, the netted gourd, and an ear of corn. He donned a ceremonial blanket, and was commissioned to deposit the *paho* in a spring. As no songs were sung, and as he bore an ear of corn and a single *paho*, one would naturally have regarded this youth as a novice, but such was not the interpretation given me by the assembly. When the youth returned, he carried spring water in the netted gourd, and still held the ear of corn. The chief took these from him and laid the netted gourd on a little pile of sacred meal near the altar. On the corn, which he deposited near by, he sprinkled sacred meal. The chief then took the pipe, lighted by the pipe-lighter, and smoked several puffs into the water, kneeling on the floor before it. He then handed the pipe to the young courier, who squatted at his side and smoked in turn.

While this was going on, another young man, who had brought into the kiva a number of willow sticks as thick as a lead pencil and perhaps two feet long, began cutting them into small sections, allowing them to fall into a basket tray. After having made these sections, he moistened them and carried the basket out of the room, placing it on the roof of the kiva, so that the moistened twigs might dry in the sun. Later, several balls of clay, about the size of baseballs, were made and placed in the same basket. These are the objects called the "frog's young," which I have described in my accounts of the Snake and Flute ceremonials at Walpi. The Antelope chief then took a flag leaf, moistened it, and made an annulet, rolling the leaf back and forth, in and out, and when finished he tied to it two small feathers. In all respects this annulet was like that carried by the Flute girls in the Flute ceremony or placed on the heads of the female lightning figures on the sand picture of the Antelope altar at Walpi. It was painted black, and one of the netted gourds was placed upon it by the side of the altar.

By this time, or about 2 oclock, all the Antelope priests had finished making their *pahos*, and laid them down, each depositing his prayer-sticks in his own basket tray, in front of the altar, as shown in plate LXXI.

The chief carefully swept the floor of the kiva, gathering up all shavings, whittlings, and fragments of herbs. This refuse was placed in a blanket, sprinkled with meal, and carried out. Shortly afterward a priest brought in all the Antelope rattles and deposited them in the corner of the kiva; all these objects are in his keeping, but each priest brought to the room all his other paraphernalia.

THE ANTELOPE DANCE

The Antelope dance at Cipaulovi took place in the larger plaza at 6.20 p. m. on August 22. A *kisi* was erected on the southern part of this open space, about halfway between the central *pahoki*, or shrine, and the arcades through which the priests came from their kivas. A plank, with a hole in it symbolizing the *sipapu*, was let into the ground immediately before the *kisi*, the entrance to which was closed with a blanket (?) or cloth.

Eleven Antelope and thirteen Snake priests took part in the Antelope dance, and at Cipaulovi, as at Walpi, the whole afternoon was consumed by them in their kivas, costuming for the public exhibition. Shortly before the priests emerged from their rooms, the Antelope chief went over to the Snake kiva, and, without ceremony, asked the Snake chief if he were ready. This was in marked contrast to the formal invitation presented at Walpi, where the Antelope priests sprinkle pinches of sacred meal in the hatchway of the Snake kiva and form a line before it.

Shortly after the return of the Antelope chief to his kiva, the eleven Antelope priests filed out of their secret room, led by their chief. They wore practically the same costume as the Antelopes of Walpi, which seems to be prescribed in all the villages.

The chief carried his *tiponi* across his left arm, and bore in one hand the bow with red horsehair attached to the string. Next to him was a man with the netted gourd, an ear of corn, and a *paho*. There was a third, who later took a position midway in the line and carried a well-filled medicine bowl. Each Antelope wore a ceremonial kilt of white cotton with embroidered ends, ornamented with raincloud symbols in red and dark green. Their faces had a line of white from the corners of the mouth to the ears, and the chin was painted black. They had zigzag lines of white on the breast, arms, and legs; fox-skins depended from their waists behind, turtle-shells were fastened back of the knee, and each was richly ornamented with shell and turquois necklaces. Every Antelope except the chief and the bearer of the medicine bowl carried two rattles. A few of the participants wore cottonwood leaves in their armlets.

The procession, headed by their chief, filed four times around the plaza, the circuit being sinistral, or with the center on the left hand, but not including the *pahoki*. As the Antelopes passed the shrine they threw a pinch of meal toward it, and as they approached the *kisi* each man dropped a pinch of sacred meal on the plank, and stamped violently upon it. At the end of the fourth circuit they formed a platoon, separated into two sections by the *kisi*, the chief standing at the extreme right. They continued shaking their rattles, but not singing, while the Snake priests made their entrance. No *kalektaka*, with a whizzer, followed the Antelope priests.

The Snake priests, headed by their chief, came shortly afterward. Their chief carried his bow with red horsehair, but had no *tiponi* or other official insignia. The Snake priests followed him, and the line made four circuits of the plaza, embracing the whole rectangle in their course. As they passed the shrine they dropped a pinch of meal upon it, and when in front of the cottonwood bower they did the same, stamping violently on the plank in the ground.

W
Y
R
G
B

ALTAR OF THE ANTELOPE PRIESTS AT CUÑOPAVI

W
Y
G
R
B

ALTAR OF THE ANTELOPE PRIESTS AT ORAIBI

As a rule the Snake priests were appareled similarly to those of Walpi, but the whole face was painted black, with white under the chin and on the neck. Their cheeks were not smeared with the micaceous hematite which gives such a hideous appearance to the Walpi performers.

After the thirteen Snake men had lined up before the eleven Antelopes, who all the time were shaking their rattles, a low song began, the Antelopes being the singers. As the song progressed the Snake men locked arms and stepped backward and forward, while two men, an Antelope and a Snake, ambled backward and forward between the lines of swaying priests. They went to the *kisi* or cottonwood bower and returned to the head of the lines several times. The Antelope priest then took from the *kisi* the wad of cornstalks and vines and put it in his mouth, as the Walpi priests do the snake. The Snake priest accompanied him, placing his left hand on the shoulder of his companion and acting as the "hugger." In this way the two men pranced slowly between the lines of swaying priests, who stepped forward and backward one step, the Antelopes singing and shaking their rattles. The carrier held the wad in his mouth like a pipe, and after a few courses he was relieved by another priest. After this was continued several times, the wad was returned to the *kisi*, the asperger sprinkled water, and the Snake and Antelope priests filed away in turn, each making circuits of the plaza. No warrior with a whizzer accompanied the procession, and although one of the Antelopes wore a garland of cottonwood leaves, he did not call out at the *kisi* the foreign words, "*Tcamahía, awahía,*" etc.

THE SNAKE RACE

On the morning of August 23, before daybreak, the Antelope priests sang their songs and consecrated the trays of *pahos* before the altar. I regret to record that I was too late to see this ceremony, although I reached the kiva before sunrise. There is every probability that the songs rendered at that time correspond with the sixteen songs, with dramatic accompaniment, which I have observed at Walpi, but as *pahos* were not made in numbers on previous days, it is not probable that a similar ceremony occurred on the other mornings.

When I arrived at the pueblo from my camp near the spring, the "Snake race" was already taking place in the valley between Cipaulovi and Cuñopavi, and all the Antelope priests were seated on the rocky ledge west of the kiva watching for the return of the racers. The race was well attended, many young men from Micoñinovi and Cipaulovi contending, and its termination was clearly visible from the mesa top. It presented no important differences from the Snake race at the other villages; the winner ran up the trail past the Antelope kiva, and the prize seemed to be simply the reputation which it gave him as a runner.

Directly after the return of the racers, a number of boys and girls, who had been standing on the edge of the lower terrace, where lies the trail along which the racers approached the pueblo, started all together to run up the hill to the town. They carried cornstalks, melons, and other objects, and many of them wore small ceremonial kilts and had their bodies decorated with various pigments. As they approached the houses men and women from the spectators ran down to meet them, and, when possible, seized the objects which the children bore. This afforded much pleasure and amusement, and closely resembled what has elsewhere been described in connection with similar races.

Directly after them came a man personating a warrior. He wore a white kilt and an antelope skin, and at intervals twirled a bullroarer or whizzer. He, unlike the winner in the race, returned to the kiva accompanied by all the other Antelope priests. They sat in a circle about the fireplace, smoking and exchanging terms of relationship. After all had smoked, beginning with the chief and ending with the pipe-lighter, each man took a pinch of ashes in his hand and remained silent, squatting on the floor. One of their number sang in a low tone, and as it continued each man turned his hand about his head several times in a circular pass, spat on the ashes, which he then cast out of the hatch. Immediately afterward a bundle of dried roots was passed about, each priest nibbling a little thereof, after which he spat on his hands and rubbed them over his chest. This ceremony was purificatory in nature.

Many *pahos* were still in the basket trays, and when the winning racer approached, the Antelope chief came out of the kiva and presented one of these to him. At the termination of the race, the warrior[1] bearing the crook deposited the feather, which he wore in his hair, on the Antelope altar.

THE SNAKE DANCE

The Snake dance at Cipaulovi, as in all the other Tusayan pueblos, took place just before sunset; it was well attended by people from the other villages, and included the four Americans in my party. The dance itself was almost identical with that at Walpi, although much smaller in the number of participants.

There were fifteen Antelope and thirteen Snake priests. When the time arrived for the dance, the chief of the Antelopes, who had been dressing in their kiva, went to the hatch of the Snake kiva and asked the Snake chief if he were ready. Immediately after his return, the Antelope priests filed out of their chamber into the plaza where the *kisi* had been erected. Their chief carried his badge of office, or *tiponi*, and he was followed by a priest holding in both hands a medicine bowl and aspergill. This man, however, did not, as in other Snake dances, wear a garland of cottonwood leaves, nor did he cry out the mystic words, "*Tcamahía*," etc., which formed such a conspicuous feature in the Walpi ceremony. There was likewise no personification of a warrior (*kalektaka*) bearing the whizzer or bullroarer.

---

[1] This was the man who stood at one of the goals in the race.

The Antelope priests made four circuits of the plaza, in the space to the southward and eastward of the shrine and *kisi*, shaking their rattles as they marched, and dropping a pinch of sacred meal in the shrine as they passed it. Each man stamped on the plank before the *kisi*, dropping meal as he did so, and then the whole line formed a platoon facing eastward, where they stood shaking their rattles.

Immediately the Snake men followed, making four circuits of the plaza, their course being much longer than that of the Antelope priests. As each priest passed before the *kisi* in these circuits, he stamped on the plank, after having dropped upon it a pinch of sacred meal. They then lined up in front of the Antelope priests, and sang songs similar to those at Walpi. There was no call, however, to the warrior gods by an asperger. Among other episodes at Cipaulovi, I missed that quivering movement of the snake whips, elsewhere described.

The line of Snake men next divided into groups of three—each trio composed of a "carrier," a "hugger," and a "gatherer." The carrier knelt down before the *kisi*, received a snake from a man within, put it in his mouth, and began the circuit of the plaza. He did not close his eyes, as do the performers at Walpi, and the hugger simply placed one hand on his shoulder. The carrier did not touch the snake, as at Oraibi, after he had placed it in his mouth; and, instead of throwing the reptile from him when he had completed the circuit, he took it out of his mouth and laid it on the ground at a certain place. The gatherer picked up the snake, not confining his attention to the carrier whom he followed, and not first throwing meal to the sun or sprinkling it on the reptile, as at Oraibi. As the carrier started on his circuit, he tucked his *paho* in his belt. The *pahos* used at Walpi were made by the Snake priests; those employed at Cipaulovi were made by the Antelope chief and given to the Snake men.

As the snake carrier left the *kisi*, in his circuit, the asperger sprinkled him with medicine, but no maidens stood near to throw prayer-meal upon them, as at Walpi. After all the snakes had been carried in the mouths of participants in the dance, the Snake chief made a circle of sacred meal about 20 feet in diameter in front of the *pahoki*, and drew in it six meal radii, corresponding to the six cardinal points. The reptiles were then thrown into this ring, and the asperger sprinkled them with medicine, after which the maidens and women threw sacred meal from their basket plaques upon the writhing mass. At a signal the Snake priests rushed to the reptiles, seized as many as they could, and, as at Walpi, departed hastily down the mesa trails and distributed them to the cardinal points. As they left the plaza, a perfect rain of spittle from the spectators on the surrounding housetops followed them.

The subsequent vomiting and feast differed in no essential particulars from the same episodes at Walpi.

There were among the spectators numerous prominent Snake men from Walpi, including Kopeli the Snake chief, Supela his father, and Saliko his mother. The former did not enter the kivas; and the last mentioned, who came to Cipaulovi the night before the dance, told me she prepared the "antidote" for the priests at Cipaulovi, as at Walpi. In essentials the public Snake dance in the pueblos last mentioned is similar, and the dress of the Snake and Antelope men practically identical. It would seem as if the ceremony were derived from Walpi rather than from Cuñopavi.

The Snake dance at Cipaulovi, as will be seen from the foregoing account, is abbreviated in character, small in number of participants, and curtailed in secret rites. On August 21 (*komoktotokya*), the day before the Antelope dance, the chief went off in search of wood, leaving his altar for a long time, with no one in the kiva for several hours. Such a proceeding may be more primitive, but it never happens at Walpi. While at Walpi the sand picture and altar of the Antelopes are prepared on the first day (*yüñya*), they are not made until the sixth or seventh day at Cipaulovi, or, more accurately speaking, the third day before the Snake dance. This in itself introduces a modification in secret ceremonials. The *awata natcis*, or bows with red horsehair, were not hung upon the ladders before the eighth day, and were first seen on the ninth; at Walpi, they were placed there on the fifth day. All ceremonials with a snake *tiponi* were obviously omitted, and there are several complicated rites at Walpi which probably are absent in the Snake villages of other Tusayan pueblos.

THE CUÑOPAVI SNAKE CEREMONY

GENERAL REMARKS

The ritual of this Tusayan village is less known than that of any other, not a single Cuñopavi ceremony ever having been described. There is, however, evidence that the complete Tusayan ritual is performed at this pueblo, and its age and isolation leads me to suspect that the modifications are of value from a comparative point of view. It is, therefore, with great pleasure that I am able, in this article, to present the results of the first study of Cuñopavi ceremonials. Unfortunately, however, I can speak only of the public Snake dance and describe the Antelope altar, since I have not witnessed any of the secret rites pertaining to the ceremony.

The attendance at the Snake dance of Cuñopavi, in 1896, consisted of ten white persons and numerous Indians from the other mesas, in addition to the inhabitants; there were also two Navahos, who had come from a long distance.

THE ANTELOPE ALTAR

The sand mosaic of the Cuñopavi Antelope altar (plate LXXII) was bordered by a margin of sand of four colors—yellow, green, red, and white, separated by black lines—and was of rectangular shape, about the size of the Walpi altar. There were but two rows of semicircular rain-cloud figures in the inclosure of the margin. The first row, adjacent the margin, had four members—yellow, green, red, and white, in sequence, beginning at the right of the row. The second series had five semicircles—yellow, black, yellow, green, and yellow, following the same sequence as the former. There were four zigzag lightning symbols, colored yellow, green, red, and white, each of which had a horn on the right side of the head. At the angles of each lightning symbol there were drawn, with black sand, figures of feathers. The zigzag lightning strokes and the semicircular rain clouds were outlined with black lines, and parallel lines representing falling rain were short and numerous. As at Cipaulovi, there were no stone implements around the margin of the sand picture, but at its four corners there were small cones of clay, each bearing the color of a cardinal point—yellow, green, red, and white, respectively. The front and rear margins of the sand picture, like those of the Cipaulovi altar, were destitute of objects. On each side of the sand picture there were four clay pedestals, two of which bore straight

287

sticks and two supported sticks crooked at the extremities. The *tiponi* was placed on a small hillock of sand somewhat back of the rear right-hand corner of the sand picture. In the rear of the left-hand corner, leaning against the wall of the kiva, were two rectangular slabs, the symbolism on which was not distinct, recalling the so-called Butterfly virgin slab of the Walpi Antelope altar. Around them were tied strings with appended *nakwákwoci*.

At the time I studied the Cuñopavi altar of the Antelopes there were finger marks on each rain cloud of the sand picture, where the chief had taken a pinch of each colored sand to carry to his field, these being symbolic of the different colored corn which he hoped would grow there.

THE SNAKE DANCE

The Snake dance at the pueblo of Cuñopavi was performed on August 24, and was the only event of this complicated observance which I witnessed. While, therefore, my observations were limited, they constitute the first ever made by an ethnologist in this interesting and little known pueblo. Seventeen Antelope and eighteen Snake priests participated in the ceremony; each Antelope carried two[1] rattles, one in each hand, and there were three small boys among the Antelope priests, one of whom could not have been more than five years of age. The youngest of the lads was naked, but painted like his elders, and when he lined up with the other Antelopes before the *kisi* he held his place without shrinking, even when the venomous rattlesnakes crawled near him, an exhibition of infantile pluck which I have never seen excelled. This is not simply want of fear through ignorance, for again and again in their songs and talks the priests pray that they may not be bitten. He must have known the power of the snakes, but the same belief which controlled his elders gave him courage. The Cuñopavi priests handled the rattlesnakes more fearlessly, if that were possible, than the participants at any of the other pueblos.

The differences noted between the events and paraphernalia of the Antelope and Snake men at Cuñopavi and the other villages were the following: In addition to cottonwood boughs the *kisi* had cornstalks in its construction and a circle of sacred meal was made about it. The costume and body painting of the Antelopes were the same as at Walpi; there was no warrior with a whizzer or bullroarer, and the asperger did not call out the invocation to the cardinal points. The kilts of the Snake priests were as a rule without rattles, and the parallel lines with which the zigzag figure of the plumed snake were marked extended across the figure. The bandolier was cylindrical, the medicine pellets few or wanting.

---

[1]This is an interesting innovation at Cuñopavi. At Walpi and Oraibi each priest carries but one rattle. These rattles are made of buckskin stretched over a pair of circular disks and fastened to a wooden handle; they contain small objects for rattles, and are painted white.

After the entrance of the Snake and Antelope men and their prelim-inary songs, which resembled those of Walpi, the Snake chief went inside the *kisi* and passed out the snakes.   Before carrying these reptiles, the Snake priests made the circuit of the plaza in trios, the carrier, hugger, and gatherer posing in the same way as when they bear the snakes.   This, of course, was subsequent to the four circuits made in line by the Snake priests when they entered the plaza and stamped on the plank before the *kisi*.   The snake carrier handled the reptile, as at Walpi, putting it in his mouth, and did not touch it after-ward with his hands, as at Oraibi; his eyes were open as at Cipaulovi and Oraibi.   The hugger simply placed his hand on the right or left shoulder of the carrier and stood behind him, not putting his arm about the carrier's neck, as at Walpi.   After all the snakes had been carried, and while they were in the gatherer's hands, the Snake priests crowded about the entrance to the *kisi*, and something occurred which was not observable to the spectators.   The circle of meal was next made some distance away; the reptiles were then thrown within it, and the women sprinkled or threw their plaques full of meal upon the snakes.   The priests then rushed in, seized the reptiles, and darted away, as elsewhere described.   As they left the plaza all of the specta-tors spat after them, as at Cipaulovi.   Then occurred something which had never before been witnessed in any of the six presentations of the Snake dance which I have observed.   Several of the Snake priests did not obtain reptiles from the writhing mass in the ring of meal, and consequently did not rush down the steep mesa trails with those who did, but they made the circuit of the plaza four times before the *kisi*, sprinkled meal on the *sipapû* and stamped on the plank, after which they filed off to their kiva.   It was not clear to me whether this was accidental or an unusual modification; but I am inclined to think that the number of reptiles was so few that these priests could not obtain any with which to rush down the mesa, and this way of retiring to their kiva is prescribed in such a case.

16 ETH——19

THE ORAIBI SNAKE CEREMONY

General Remarks

On account of the isolation of the pueblo and the persistent way in which its people have resisted innovations, the presentation of the snake ritual at Oraibi has long been regarded as the most primitive of all the Hopi ceremonials.

In an article[1] on the "Ancient Province of Tusayan," Major Powell partially described an Oraibi ceremony, but too briefly to be identified. So far as I know this was the first account of Tusayan kiva rites. A large oil painting of a Tusayan ceremony and altar has long hung in the pottery court of the National Museum. This painting, I am informed by Major Powell, was made under his direction and represents a scene in a Tusayan kiva. Several priests, apparently engaged in rites about a medicine bowl, are figured, and from the arrangement of the maize of different colors about it I suppose the picture represents the making of charm liquid. The attitude of the priest in the act of blowing smoke into the bowl confirms me in this interpretation.

The representation of the reredos is unlike anything which has been reported from Tusayan. The room has a hatchway, but is unlike any Oraibi kiva which I have seen.

In 1895 I figured and described[2] the altar of one of the Flute societies at Oraibi. Mr H. R. Voth, a resident missionary, has recently given much time to the study of the Oraibi ritual, and has shown me several sketches of highly characteristic altars, accounts of which he intends later to publish. We are, therefore, on the way to a more exact knowledge of the ceremonials, religious paraphernalia, and altars of this interesting pueblo which has so long resisted the efforts of ethnologists.

The Antelope Altar

The Antelope priests at Oraibi were not overgenial to strangers wishing to pry into their secret rites, and the Snake priests positively refused to allow me or any white man, except the missionary, Mr Voth, to enter their kiva.[3] I entered the Antelope kiva uninvited, but my

---

[1] Scribner's Magazine, Vol. XI, No. 2, New York, December, 1875.

[2] The Oraibi Flute Altar; Journal of American Folk-lore, Vol. VIII, Oct.–Dec., 1895.

[3] One or two white men told me that they ventured into the Snake kiva when the priests were away and saw nothing there but stone images, probably twins, or the Little War Gods. As the Snake chief at Oraibi has no *tiponi*, he makes no altar, and the stone image was the tutelary god of warriors, known as the Little Gods of War, Püükoñhoya and Palunhoya.

Entrance and circuit of the Antelope priests

Entrance of the Snake priests

THE ANTELOPE DANCE AT ORAIBI

Platoons of Antelope and Snake priests at the opening of the dance

Snake priests shaking their whips

THE ANTELOPE DANCE AT ORAIBI

presence there was not welcome, and most of the half hour which I spent there was occupied in reasoning with the priests. I succeeded in making a sketch of their altar, but was several times ordered out, and was therefore not loth to leave the kiva when I had finished. There was some little satisfaction in being able to tell the priests of Oraibi in their own kiva that my studies of Antelope altars in other pueblos enabled me to interpret about every object which theirs possessed, since they were so similar. This, however, was not strictly true as regards all the fetishes, for there were two or three objects on the Antelope altar at Oraibi which are different from those at Walpi, Cipaulovi, and Cuñopavi, and beyond my comprehension.

The size of the Antelope altar at Oraibi (plate LXXIII) was about the same as that of Walpi, and the sand picture almost identical, so that a description of this portion of it would be a duplication of accounts elsewhere published.[1] The sand picture was surrounded by a yellow, green, red, and white border of sand. There were semicircular figures of rain clouds in yellow, green, red, and white, arranged in the same order as at Walpi, and in like sequence. The four lightning symbols, however, differed somewhat, all of these having square appendages to the heads, instead of horns and diagonally marked rectangles. These square appendages, as nearly as I could make out, were on both sides of the heads, but accuracy in this minute particular was next to impossible. There were no stone hoes about the border of the sand picture, as at Walpi. Along each side was a row of clay pedestals, in each of which were inserted straight or crooked sticks, to the tops of which were attached red-stained *nakwákwocis*. They were arranged side by side and there were no breaks or "gateways," as at Walpi. At the side of each crook a small netted gourd was placed. At the end of each line of sticks, one on each side of the altar, there was a head of an antelope, with horns, nose, and neck. These objects are not found on the Antelope altars of Walpi, Cipaulovi, or Cuñopavi, and are significant accessories in the secret ceremonials.

The floor in front of the altar had no pedestals with upright sticks, but upon it was a medicine bowl, the six-directions corn, and an aspergill.

The rear of the altar was strikingly different from that of any Antelope altar which has been described. There were no stone fetishes of animals, as at Walpi, and although the two *tiponis* were present, both of these belonged to the Antelopes. The Snake society at Oraibi, as at Cipaulovi and Cuñopavi, has no palladium or *tiponi*. These two objects stood just in the rear of the margin of the sand picture, one on each side of a square medicine bowl, which occupied the middle and therefore corresponds in position to the mountain-lion fetish on the Walpi altar. Projecting from the top of the left-hand *tiponi* was an object which, from my point of observation, resembled a stone implement, but

---

[1] Jour. Amer. Eth. and Archæol., Vol. IV, pp. 17-24.

in other respects the two *tiponis* resembled those of the Walpi altar. *Pahos* were placed upright near each *tiponi*, and from one of these a long string, with feathers tied to the extremity, was stretched across the sand picture.

The medicine bowl back of the altar had three T-shape figures painted upon it, and behind this vessel there were four *pahos* placed upright with strings drawn over the top of the medicine bowl. At the extreme left of the rear of the altar there was an ancient vase with terraced elevations. Back of all the objects at the rear of the altar there was a ridge of sand in which was inserted a row of eagle wing feathers. Between the rows of crooks and the lateral margin of the sand picture long *pahos* were laid lengthwise on the floor. A basket of sacred meal was placed on the floor near the right-hand effigy of an antelope head.

It will be seen from an examination of the details of the Antelope altar of Oraibi and comparison with those of Cipaulovi, Cuñopavi, and Walpi, that it is the most complicated and has several objects not elsewhere duplicated. Moreover, the arrangement of the objects back of the altar is such that it would be quite strange, indeed almost impossible, for the Antelope chief to introduce several of the events which occur in the sixteen-song celebration at Walpi.

THE ANTELOPE DANCE

The Antelope or Corn dance at Oraibi took place at sunset, as in the other villages, but it was not so brilliant a spectacle nor was it performed by so many priests as at Walpi. The Antelope priests, headed by their chief, marched directly from their kiva to the *kisi*, and made four circuits of the plaza, each priest stamping on the depressed plank as he passed before it.

After they had formed a platoon, the Antelope chief drew a line of meal in front of them, and at the extreme end of this line he set his *tiponi* upright on the ground. At one side of this badge, also on the line of meal, the asperger deposited his medicine bowl. Each Antelope then placed the netted gourd and stick which he carried on the ground before him, so that all these objects were arranged in a row before the platoon of Antelope priests.

The Snake men came out of their kiva and made four circuits of the plaza in front of the line of Antelope priests, who shook their rattles as the Snakes passed before them. Each Snake priest dropped a pinch of meal and stamped vigorously on the plank as he passed the *kisi*, and then took his place in line before the platoon of Antelope priests. They were led by their chief, an old man, who, however, had no badge of office on his arm. The Antelope priests wore feathers in their hair and a small white feather on the crown of the head. The asperger was distinguished by a fillet of cottonwood leaves. Their bodies were painted with zigzag lines in white, but all wore heavy shell and turquois necklaces. Each priest, except the asperger, carried a rattle in the right hand and a stick and water gourd in the left.

The chief bore his *tiponi* over his left arm. All wore white dance kilts with rain-cloud decorations, and a characteristic sash. Several had bandoliers of yarn over the right shoulder and a hank of wool on the left knee, but none of the Antelope priests wore moccasins and but few had fox-skins dangling from their belts. The position of the chief was at the extreme right of the line. An old Antelope priest carried an ear of corn.

Each of the Snake priests wore a small red feather in his hair, but their faces were not painted; all, however, had daubs of white pigment on their arms and legs. Several had hastily tied white kilts, similar to those of the Antelopes, about their loins, and only two had the characteristic snake kilts. Each carried his snake whip in his right hand, a bag of meal in his left, and most of the performers wore moccasins. None had necklaces, fox-skins, or bandoliers. The platoon of Snake men stood some distance from the Antelopes, with a lad on the extreme right. As the Antelopes sang and shook their rattles, the Snake men bent slightly forward, pointing their whips toward the ground, then moving them backward and forward with a waving motion. As the music continued, the asperger, not leaving his position by the side of the Antelope chief, called out in a low voice the words "*Tcamahia,*" etc, several times.

After he had ceased, he went to the opening of the *kisi,* and took out one of the bundles of cornstalks, melons, and other vines, put the butt in his mouth, holding the other end in both hands before him. A second priest, putting his left hand on the left shoulder of the asperger, walked behind the carrier, stroking his back with a snake whip. In this way the two made several promenades between the platoons of Snake and Antelope priests, the former singing and shaking their rattles, all with netted gourds and sticks in their left hands. As this proceeding continued the Snake priests stepped backward and forward in line, poising themselves first on one leg and then on the other.

At the conclusion of this dance the Snake priests filed about the plaza, making the circuits before the *kisi,* and returned to their kiva. The Antelope priests did the same, but went to their own ceremonial chamber. This closed *totokya* (August 18), so far as public ceremonies were concerned.

THE SNAKE RACE

A snake race of Oraibi took place at sunrise of the same day on which the Snake dance was celebrated, as at Walpi, Cipaulovi, and Cuñopavi.

THE SNAKE DANCE

At a short time before sunset, on August 19, the Antelope priests filed out of their kiva and made four circuits in front of the *kisi,* each stamping on the plank and dropping a pinch of meal as he passed. They were headed by the chief, who carried his *tiponi* on his left forearm. The chief in turn was followed by the asperger, who wore a chaplet of cottonwood leaves and carried a medicine bowl and aspergill with both hands. Each Antelope wore a white "breath-feather" in his hair, which hung down his back, but none had a bunch of feathers on his head. The chin was painted black and there was a white line along the upper border of the black from ear to ear across the upper lip. All wore necklaces of shell or turquois and each was adorned with zigzag lines of white pigment along the body, on each breast, from shoulder to belt, continued on the back on each side to the waist. There were also zigzag white lines on the arm, and the forearm was painted white. Each wore a bandolier of woolen yarn over the right shoulder, and everyone, save the asperger, carried a rattle in the right hand. All the dancers wore kilts and embroidered sashes, with pendent fox-skins behind, and all had moccasins. Thus appareled they lined up in a platoon, the chief at the left, the *kisi* midway in the line, shaking their rattles while awaiting the Snake priests.

The Snake priests then came from their kiva headed by their chief, who had no *tiponi*. Each Snake priest wore a bunch of feathers in his hair, and curious feathered objects on the back of the head. Their faces were blackened, but there was no white paint on the chin. All wore shell and turquois necklaces, armlets, and wristlets, and daubs of white on their foreheads, breasts and backs.

Their kilts were colored red, with zigzag figures of the plumed snake, bearing tripod-shape and alternate parallel bars as ornaments. Less than half their number had a fringe of antelope hoofs on the lower edge of the kilt; all wore fox-skins pendent from their loins, turtle-shell rattles on the leg, moccasins stained red with sesquioxide of iron, and red wristlets. Each carried a snake whip. After the preliminary forward and backward steps, and after shaking their whips in unison with the songs of the Antelopes, they divided into groups of three, called carrier, hugger, and gatherer.

The snakes are carried at Oraibi in a way peculiar to this pueblo and differently from that adopted in any other Tusayan village. The posture of the hugger is likewise exceptional. When the carrier approaches the *kisi* in which the snakes are confined, he places his whip in his belt, seizes the reptile, puts its neck in his mouth, with head pointing to his left, and grasps the body of the snake with his two hands, the right above the left. The carrier does not close his eyes, and he takes but one reptile at a time. In this way he ambles about the plaza in a circle, the center toward his left. When he has completed the circuit, he takes the reptile from his mouth and lays it on the ground, with the head pointing away from the *kisi*. The hugger follows the carrier, placing his left hand on the left shoulder of the carrier, whose back he strokes with the snake whip. He stands behind the carrier, and not at his side, as at Walpi. The gatherer picks up the reptiles after they have been placed on the ground. If the reptile coils for defense, he strives to make him uncoil by movements of the whip; otherwise he takes a little sacred meal, says a prayer, casts a pinch to the setting sun, sprinkles a little on the head of the reptile, and suddenly grasps the snake back of the head. The gatherers collect the snakes whenever dropped by the carriers, and hold them in their hands as the others are borne about the plaza.

The women did not stand in line and sprinkle the Snake priests with meal as they passed with their burdens, but when the reptiles were thrown in a heap, after the dance, both maids and matrons emptied trays of meal upon the snakes on the ground.

After all the reptiles had been carried about the plaza in the way indicated above, they were thrown in the middle of a ring of sacred meal, marked with six radii, also of meal, corresponding to the cardinal points, the zenith, and the nadir. At a signal the Snake priests rushed to the circle, seized all the snakes they could gather, and darted off with them down the mesa sides to the four quarters, where the reptiles were deposited. Later they returned, divested themselves of their scanty clothing, retired to a secluded spot, bathed, took an emetic (?), and vomited. The Antelopes meanwhile made four circuits in front of the *kisi* and retired to their kiva. As at Walpi, the Snake men feasted at nightfall, not having tasted food on the day of the dance.

In reviewing the details of the Snake dance at Oraibi, as described above, we are impressed, first, with the small number of participants, eleven Antelope and fifteen Snake priests; secondly, with the peculiar manner of carrying the reptiles; and, thirdly, with the lack of brilliancy in the personal adornment of the performers. The entrance of the Snake chief, Kopeli, at Walpi, followed by his band, is a most striking affair, full of life and startling in character. At Oraibi this part is very tame in comparison, without dash or excitement, and fails in vigor, energy, and power. The number of participants at Oraibi, not a third of those at Walpi, is also disappointing to one who has seen the dance at the East Mesa. I can, however, well believe that the Oraibi Snake dance more closely resembles that of Walpi before the advent of so many visitors, than does the present exhibition at the latter pueblo. Everything at Walpi shows a vigorous cult, a popular society, an earnestness as great as at Oraibi, but the primitive character of the whole is somewhat spoiled by the introduction of gaudy ribbons, ornaments, and personal decorations purchased from the trader.

DIFFERENCES IN ACCESSORIES

General Remarks

The most striking differences in such events as were witnessed in the Snake dance presentations thus far recorded have been noted in the preceding pages. None of them are of sufficient importance to indicate more than local modifications. The strong likenesses which one ceremony bears to the other indicate the same cult and a common origin.

It would, I believe, be a little short of puerile to ascribe the Snake ceremonials in the different Tusayan pueblos to independent evolutions, so close are their similarities in details and so definite are the legends of their common origin. There is, however, an aspect of the study of Snake dances among other pueblos which merits more serious attention, to the intelligent discussion of which exact data on the Tusayan variants may be of value. From a study of the amount of variation in the same rite in these five pueblos, we may obtain a knowledge of the limits of variants which will be of service in comparative studies.

The following are some of the features in the Snake ceremonies which, I am told, did not occur at Oraibi[1] and Cipaulovi:

I. The singing of a series of sixteen songs on the first four days.

II. The personification of the bear and puma, and accompanying rites.

III. Ceremonial mixing of Snake medicine.

As there was no Snake altar at Oraibi, Cipaulovi, or Cuñopavi, the reptiles were not thrown across the room, but simply dried on the sand, as at Sia.

Both at Oraibi and Cipaulovi, *pahos* of different lengths corresponding to different days and distance of shrines were not made, and as this is a prominent feature in the Walpi variant, its absence has profoundly modified the attendant rites at the other villages, imparting to them many modifications.

Pahos

Most of the *pahos* or prayer-sticks made at Cipaulovi on the day before the Snake dance were of the length of the middle finger, while at Walpi they are of the length of the ultimate joint. One of the component sticks has a flat facet, whereas at Walpi neither has a face. The stick with a facet upon it is the female; the other, the male.

---

[1]Mr H. R. Voth has made elaborate studies of the secret rites of the Oraibi Snake dance, from beginning to end. His observations, when published, will no doubt throw a flood of light on the unknown portions of the ceremonial.

Of all the suggestions that have been offered to explain the *paho* on comparative grounds, none seem to me more worthy of acceptance than that it is a sacrifice by symbolic substitute. The folktales of the Pueblos are not without reference to human sacrifice, and offerings of corn or meal would be natural among an agricultural people like the Hopi. Substitutes for human sacrifices to the gods were sometimes made by the Aztecs in the form of dough images, so that the method by substitution, common in Europe, was not unknown in America. When occasion demanded, the Hopi legend says, they sacrificed a child and their chief, but in these days sacrifice has come to be a symbolic substitute of products of the field—corn, flour, or *pahos*—still retaining, however, the names "male" and "female," and with a human face painted on one end of the prayer-stick.

The Kisi

Each of the four pueblos of Tusayan where the Snake dance is celebrated has a *kisi* or bower made of cottonwood boughs, near which the Snake dance is celebrated, and in which the reptiles are confined before they are carried about the plaza. These *kisis* are all very similar in their construction, the only difference which I have detected being the use of cornstalks[1] and reeds with the cottonwood boughs in the Oraibi celebration. All were closed in front by a wagon-sheet or cloth.

The *kisi* at Oraibi is placed in the open space west of the town, that of Cipaulovi in the main plaza, and that of Cuñopavi in the plaza between the westernmost and inner row of houses. The vicinity of the *kisi* to a shrine is peculiar to Cipaulovi.

Snake Whips

The snake whips of the Middle Mesa pueblos are made of two sticks instead of one, as at Walpi, and in some instances have attached packets of cornhusk, presumably containing prayer-meal, which are absent on the Walpi snake whips. These may thus be regarded as true *pahos* or prayer-sticks. The neat little fringed bags of buckskin, in which the Snake priests of Walpi carry their sacred meal, I did not see at Cipaulovi or Oraibi, where the meal bags were large and coarse.

Snake Kilts

The snake kilts vary in no important detail in the different villages, except that they are sometimes made of deer or antelope skin, sometimes of cloth, but are always stained red. The zigzag figure in the middle of the kilt is decorated with crossbars alternating with tripod figures, or simple parallel lines. The kilts of the Middle Mesa and Oraibi generally have these bars extending across the figure of the

---

[1] In the Sia variant cornstalks are said to be used in the construction of the "grotto," which Mrs Stevenson describes as "a conical structure of cornstalks bearing ripe fruit." This "grotto" I regard as the Sia equivalent of the Tusayan *kisi*.

snake.   The lower fringe may be of tin cones or antelope hoofs, or they may be destitute of all appendages, according to the pueblo.   Tin cones are universal at Walpi.

The feathers on the heads of the Snake priests vary in the different pueblos, especially those hanging downward on the hair behind.   The antelope kilts are similar, and the sashes, fox-skins, and belts identical. The other striking differences have been mentioned in the account of the dance in each pueblo.

The absence at Cipaulovi, Cuñopavi, and Oraibi of the personifica-tion of the *kalektaka*, or warrior, who carries the bow and arrow, and who twirls the whizzer, is noteworthy.   At Walpi this personage appears in the rear of the line of Antelopes as they enter the plaza, then stands at the extreme left of the platoon, and is the last to leave the *kisi* at the close of the dance.   He uses the whizzer at critical times in the ceremony, and has appeared in the three Walpi Snake dances which I have witnessed.   He was not, however, seen in any of the vil-lages where this ceremony was celebrated in 1896.

Line of Antelope priests

The asperger carrying the wad of cornstalks and bean vines

THE ANTELOPE DANCE AT ORAIBI

Entrance of the Antelope priests

Circuit of the Antelope priests before the kisi

THE SNAKE DANCE AT ORAIBI

THEORETIC DEDUCTIONS

When we attempt to analyze the Tusayan ritual, we are led to suspect that the similarities in the great ceremonials are in part results of composition. The Tusayan people have been made up of increments, which have gradually assimilated, as history and legends describe. Each of these additions brought its own ceremonials, some of which were still practiced, and have been transmitted to descendants, surviving to the present day. The ritual has thus come to be one of composition, not of replacement.

Christianity had a like reception when it came among the pueblos. It was engrafted on the Pagan system, and so long as it was not thought to be aggressive it was welcomed; but so soon as the new cult sought to replace existing rites, it encountered resistance. Each priesthood held that its rites were efficacious, and those of associate societies were likewise good; but when any one of these priesthoods declared those of another bad, a position which to their minds was illogical, since the priests of one fraternity do not know the secret rites of another, an unusual condition arose. As history shows, there was no objection to Christianity at its advent, and it took its place with numerous Tusayan cults, in their system; but the attempt to overthrow the latter led to the hostilities which culminated in 1700.

The several components which formed the Tusayan people practiced ceremonials similar in general character, but different in details. As they became united, each retained certain of its ceremonials, which have been transmitted to our time. The similarities we detect show how close these components were.

The comparative studies of the Snake presentation which I have made in the three pueblos that celebrate this drama in the even years have led me to the conclusion that in my previous publications sufficient emphasis has not been placed on the corn worship which runs through it. The recognition of this element I owe more especially to studies of the Flute ceremonials, which, as I have insisted, are in many respects akin to the Snake dances.

As will be seen by a study of the altars of the Antelope priests, they are destitute of any idol, so that no clew can be obtained from that source in regard to the deity addressed. There are in each, however, figures of rain clouds, which prove, so far as they go, the correctness of the belief that rain worship is at least one of the most prominent features. The fetish of the War god in the Snake kiva of Oraibi is evidently a special feature as a guardian of warriors, and of small significance in a broad discussion of the meaning of the Snake dance.

Looking over the participants in the secret ceremonials of the Antelope kiva of Walpi, there are but two celebrants whom we can identify as personators. The Antelope priests, save possibly their chief, are simply celebrants, but the boy and girl who stand in the corners of the kiva must be something more; they represent some personage, and consequently I have reflected on their identity. The names given me for these two children are the Snake-youth and the Snake-maid. These names are, I believe, simply cultus-hero names applied to them because of the societies which celebrate the rites. Who the Snake-boy really is I am not yet prepared to say, but I think the Snake-maid is simply a personation of the Corn-maid, and these are my reasons for that belief:

A supernatural being or mythological conception may be represented by Hopi priests in several ways. There are three methods which occur to me—(1) a symbolic picture, (2) an image, and (3) a personification by a man, woman, or child. Designs on the reredos of altars, sand mosaics, altar slabs, and the like, are examples of the first. The rain clouds on the Antelope sand picture, the painted sun disks in the *Palülükonti* screen drama, are symbolic of the supernaturals which they represent. Images likewise represent certain gods; but they are not the gods, only symbols in graven forms, as figures are symbolic pictures. The third and highest form are personifications by men, women, or children. When necessity compels, or for practical reasons, these personifications are simply represented by symbols, effigies, or idols. Instead of a man representing the sun, we have a painted disk. This is carried out in different presentations of the same ceremony accordingly as it is elaborated or abbreviated. Thus, in one presentation of the *Mamzráuti* a woman was dressed like a certain goddess, but in another this personification was replaced by a picture of this supernatural on a board; both had the same name, both the same intent. Practical reasons led to a personification in one and a symbolic picture in the other presentation of the ceremony.

Bearing this thought in mind, let us return to a study of the Snake-maiden. When we compare her with other personifications in the Tusayan ritual, we find she is clothed in precisely the same manner, wears the same symbols, and in every way is identical with the girls in the Flute ceremony; she is, in fact, the same personage. Our studies, therefore, naturally lead us to ask who the girls of the Flute ceremony represent. We have more to guide us in this search.

The girls in the Flute are called the *Lenya-manas*, or Flute-maids, a name applied also to certain figurines on the Flute altars. This name is likewise a sacerdotal totem name of cultus heroes or tutelary deities of a Flute society.

The images of the Flute-maids on the altar represent the Corn or Germ maids. Of that there is proof, because they are sometimes called by that name and they have figures of corn painted on their bodies. Images of the same, highly elaborated into dolls, are known by the secular name, *Calako* (Corn) maids. These dolls have characteristic symbols on the cheeks, the same rain-cloud ornaments on the head, a figure of an ear of corn on the forehead, eyes of different color, and painted chins. A *Calako-mana* is the same as the effigy of the Flute-maid on the Flute altars, only with another name. In the *Lálakonti* she is called the *Lakone*-maid, and in the *Mamzráuti* the *Mamzráu*-maid, indicative of the society on whose altars they stand, just as the *Lenya*-maid in the *Lenya* or Flute society. All are special names of the same personage, the Corn-maid, *Müiyinwú*, the Mother of Germs.

In the secret ceremonials of the Flute it is not practicable to have a personification of the Corn-maid standing for nine days and nights near the altar, and she is therefore represented by an effigy, which is the image spoken of. But it is not desirable that the uninitiated should see this image, consequently it is not brought out on the plaza in public ceremonials. For this reason, at that time the girls personify the Corn-maids. Hence the two maids in the Flute ceremonials represent the same supernaturals as the images. They are the Corn-maids of legends, the Germ-girls, the Mothers of Germs, *Müiyinwú*. If the *Lenya-manas* are the Corn-maids, then *Tcüa-mana*, the Snake virgin, *Lakone-mana*, the *Lakone* virgin, and *Mamzráu-mana* are the same. The girl in the Antelope dramatization is therefore a Corn-goddess.

Let us see if the theory that the *Tcüa-mana* and the *Lenya-mana* are Corn-goddesses is supported on other grounds.

The Snake-maid in the dramatization[1] holds a bowl, stalks of corn, and bean vines; the Flute girls carry flat wooden slats, called corn *pahos*, on which corn is depicted. The chins of both are blackened, like the image of the *Lakone-mana*, Corn-maid. The entrance of the Flute girls into the town on the ninth day of the Flute ceremony corresponds, according to legends, with the entrance of the Corn-maids. The Snake-maids whom Tiyo is reported to have brought from the underworld, personified by the *Tcüa-mana* in the Antelope rites, wore clouds on her head, as do the images of the Flute maids and the girls who personate the *Lakone-mana* in the public dance. She brought all kinds of corn; so likewise the various others with whom she is identical. The so-called Snake-maid is, therefore, simply one of the Corn-maids, and the dramatization[2] in the Antelope kiva at Walpi is connected with her worship.

In ancient ceremonies we may conjecture that the gods were personified in the kivas by men or women dressed in an appropriate way and bearing prescribed symbols. In course of time, however, for practical or other reasons, images or symbolic pictures were substituted for

---

[1] Journ. Amer. Eth. and Archæol., Vol. IV, pp. 69, 76. The cornstalks and bean vines are carried in the bowl called the *patne*, q. v.

[2] Journ. Amer. Eth. and Archæol., Vol. IV, pp. 76–81.

personifications. The secret ceremonials of the Antelopes are still in that archaic condition, and the Corn-maid is still represented at Walpi by a girl of the pueblo. In the Flute rites, however, the Germ-maids or Corn-maids are represented in the secret ceremonials by effigies on the altar, and in the public part of the dance by persons—maidens of certain prescribed clans.

In the *Lálakonti* we have the same images of Corn-maids as on the Flute altars, and personifications of the same by girls in the public dance. In the *Mamzráuti* the conditions are the same as in the *Lálakonti*.

Were it desirable to extend our comparisons beyond the boundaries of Tusayan to Cibola, we should there find the personifications taken by maids representing the Corn-maids in the *Klahewey* and *Hamponey*, as I have elsewhere[1] described.

By a similar course of reasoning by which we have determined the identity of *Tcüa-mana* (Snake virgin), *Lenya-mana* (Flute virgin), *Lakone-mana* (*Lakone*-virgin), and *Mamzráu-mana* (*Mamzráu*-virgin), the associate male or boy, called *Tcüa-tiyo*, *Lenya-tiyo*, *Lakone-tiyo*, and *Mamzraú-tiyo* would also appear to be society names of the same personage. In the Walpi Snake-Antelope ceremony he carries a reptile; in the Micoñinovi Flute altar his effigy bears a flute; in the Walpi *Lálakonti* he is *Cotokinunwû*, a Sky god. The only intimation of his identity would seem to be suggested by the last mentioned. He is the renowned cultus hero appearing in different guises in these four ceremonials. In one of the variants of the Snake legend, however, he is called White-corn, an attributal name, no doubt, which varies in the different ceremonials or religious fraternities.

Two variants of the legend of the Snake society have been published which apparently differ very greatly, but which in essentials are similar, although neither of these pretends to be accurate in details. In the variant first referred to,[2] one of seven brothers, named from different colored corn, sought and found a maiden in a cave inhabited by Snake people, under guidance of a snake. These maidens were dancing, and the great snake chief "took hold of a cloudy substance," and began pulling, when a girl, "Bright-eyes," emerged, and was given to him as a wife. Under her direction, "White-corn," the youth, sought his home, and his bride was known as *Tcüawüqti*. When they joined his kindred, it was "noticed" (recognized) that in times of drought her prayers for rain were efficacious. The people desired her to erect the rain-cloud altar of her native home, to which she replied, "Not until a child is born." She later conceived (in a tempest), and the people were glad, because they hoped for a rain chief. White-corn and his wife retired to a distant mesa, and after seven days returned with her offspring, seven reptiles. The people sought in their disappointment to

[1] Journ. Amer. Eth. and Archæol., Vol. I, pp. 46–55.

[2] Legend of the Snake order of the Hopi as told by outsiders. Journ. American Folk-lore, Vol. I, 1888. Snake ceremonials at Walpi; Journ. Amer. Eth. and Archæol., Vol. IV, 1894.

kill the brood, but an old man took them with the mother and father to his house. Something of unknown character happened in that house, and the Snake-woman, her offspring, and the old man vanished. The old man came back alone; the Snake-woman never returned. There are many details which I have omitted, but the essentials to which I would call attention are that a young man, after many adventures, found in a cave inhabited by Snake people a maid, whom he brought to the home of his own kin. She gave birth to reptiles and disappeared. The name of the young man was White-corn; the Snake-maid was associated with rain clouds.

The incidents of the second variant are more detailed. I need not mention them, but will restrict my account to the main outline.

A youth, under guidance of Spider-woman, visited the underworld and had many adventures with several mythic beings. He entered a room where people were clothed in snake skins, and was initiated into mysterious ceremonials, in which he learned prayers which bring corn and rain. He received two maids, associated with clouds, who knew the songs and prayers efficacious to bring rains. He carried them to the upper world to his own people. One, the Snake-woman, he married; the other became the bride of the Flute-youth. His wife gave birth to reptiles. He left them and their mother, and migrated to another country.[1]

When we examine the legend of this youth, Tiyo, and his adventures in search of the two maids, we see still other evidences of the germ-worship or corn-worship referred to above. In the Snake kiva of the other world the chief told him, " Here we have abundance of rain and corn; in your land there is but little; so thus shall you use the *nahú* [charm liquid to bring them]; fasten these prayers in your breast; and these are the songs you shall sing, and these the *pahos* you shall make (for that purpose); and when you display the white [zigzag lines of kaolin] and the black on your bodies, the clouds will come." When the chief gave Tiyo portions of the different colored sands from the altar, he said, "These are the colors of the corn Tiyo's prayers will bring"—that is, symbols of corn. He gave the two corn-rain maids[2] into Tiyo's keeping—one for himself and one for his younger brother (presumably the Flute chief).

I believe, however, we should not seek to identify too minutely the details of myths or legends in ceremonial proceedings, for undoubtedly the Hopi variants are more or less distorted, changed, and otherwise modified in recital, translation, and transmittal.

The main points are, however, comparable; a cultus hero sought a mythic land blessed with abundance, and brought from that favored place the corn-rain maids, whose worship was powerful in bringing food and rain.

---

[1] Journ. Amer. Eth. and Archæol., Vol. IV, pp. 106–119.

[2] These maids were enveloped by white fleecy clouds; the effigies of the Corn-maids have symbols of clouds on their heads.

Stripped of poetic embellishment, the legend has a practical interpretation.   The two necessities, corn and rain, failed the ancient Hopi
at some early epoch in their history, so that they were in danger of
starvation, when one of their number, furnished with prayer offerings
as sacrifices, sought other people who knew prayers, songs, and rites to
bring the desired gifts.   In order to learn these charms, he was initiated
into their priesthood by this foreign people, and to make that adoption
complete, married one of their maids, and, to save his brethren, he
brought his bride and offspring to live with his own people.   Her
children were like those of her family (the Snake clan) and unlike
his, and hence trouble arose between them.   The mother returned to
her own land and the father also sought a new home.   Their children
inherited the prayers and songs which bring corn and rain, and they
were ancestors of the present Snake people.[1]

So it is, I believe, that every year, when the proper time comes, the
men of the Snake family who have been initiated into the Snake
fraternity, and the descendants to whom these prayers, songs, and
fetishes were transmitted, assemble, and in order that their work may
resemble the ancestral, and thus be more efficacious, they gather the
reptiles from the fields, dance with them as of old, personating their
"mother," the Corn and Mist maids, in the kiva dramatization, and at
the close of the dance say their prayers in hearing of the reptiles that
they may repeat them to higher deities.   In other words, they strive to
imitate the conditions, so far as possible, which tradition ascribes to
that favored place of the Snake people, where corn is plentiful and
rain abundant.   The worship of a Great Snake plays no part, but the
dance is simply the revival of the worship of the Snake people as
legends declare it to have been practiced when Tiyo was initiated
into its mysteries in the world which he visited.

In the same way we may explain the Flute observance as a ceremony
for the fructification of corn and production of rain.   The Flute-youth
also obtained as his bride a Corn-mist maid.   Her children were not
serpents, but ancestral members of the Flute clans, and when the
descendants celebrate their dance, representatives of her people take
part.

The nucleus of the Hopi confederacy is said to have been formed by
a consolidation of these two phratries, the Snakes and the Flutes, who
are reputed to be of the same blood, since their mothers were of the
same people.   But the mother of the Snake people, *Tcüawuqti*, in olden
time gave birth to reptiles, the elder brothers of Snake men.   Striving
to reproduce the ancestral ceremonials, representatives of the legendary
participants are introduced, and these are the reptiles which are

---

[1]Notwithstanding strong claims are made to the contrary for other societies, I think there is evidence of an intimate relationship between the Snake priesthood and the Snake phratry, as I have already
elsewhere shown. This conclusion is likewise supported by Hodge's study of the Keresan and
Tanoan clans. There are, of course, many priests in the Snake fraternity at Walpi from other
phratries, but the majority, including the chief, are from the Snake people.

gathered into the kivas. They are washed,[1] because everyone who takes part in a ceremony must first bathe as a purification.

While this theory of the Snake dance is plausible, it offers no explanation of why the reptiles are carried in the mouths of the priests. It can readily be seen that it presupposes that they dance in the plaza with the priests, but why are they not simply carried in the hands? For this I confess I have no adequate explanation, but the fact that they are carried in the hands as well as in the mouths at Oraibi is suggestive, especially if the Oraibi celebration is the most primitive. If we suppose that the Oraibi method is intermediate in development between that of Walpi and the ancestral, we may suppose that formerly the participants danced with the snakes in their hands. Some daring priest, for a sensation, still holding the reptile in this way, put its neck in his mouth, possibly to prevent its coiling and hiding its size. That method was startling and was adopted by all, a condition which persists at Oraibi. A further evolution of the custom would be the removal of the hands, when the reptile would be carried wholly in the mouth, as at Walpi, Cipaulovi, and Cuñopavi.[2]

We have knowledge of pueblo peoples where the custom of carrying reptiles in the hands still persists, or survived to within a few years, but that does not prove that Tusayan derived its dance from that source. The participants in the Keresan Snake dances probably did not carry the reptiles in their mouths. In Espejo's reference to the Acoma variant, in 1583, no mention is made of this startling method of handling reptiles, and it would hardly have escaped mention had it been noticed, as it must have been had it existed. Mrs Stevenson, in her valuable account of the Snake dance of Sia, does not mention the custom of putting the snake in the mouth, but speaks of the Sia priests as carrying them in their hands. The Hopi claim that the Keresan priests never put the reptiles in their mouths. Thus the evidence, such as it is, seems to point to the conclusion that the habit was locally developed in Tusayan.

The public exhibition, called the Antelope dance, on the afternoon of the eighth day, is evidently connected with corn celebrations, for at that time a wad of cornstalks and melon vines, instead of the reptiles, is carried in the mouths of the priests, as on the following day.

The episode in the Snake kiva at Walpi, when the bear and puma personators carried cornstalks in their mouths and moved them before the faces of men, women, and children spectators, has probably the same significance.[3] The pinches of different colored sand which were taken from the sand picture of the Antelopes before it was dismantled were carried to the cornfields, as symbolic of the different colored corn they hoped their prayers would bring conformably to the legend of its efficacy in that direction.

---

[1] Journ. Amer. Eth. and Archæol., Vol. IV, pp. 81–86.
[2] The same method appears to have existed elsewhere. American Anthropologist, Vol. VI, No. 3, 1893.
[3] Journ. Amer. Eth. and Archæol., Vol. IV, pp. 62, 63.

While this bifid element of corn worship and rain ceremonials runs through the whole festival, that part of it which pertains to rain-making is most prominent in the work of the Snake priests, while corn rites pertain to the Antelopes. The two elements are interwoven, but, as would naturally be the case, the corn rites are most prominent in the kiva celebrations of the Antelope priests. The Antelope chief controls the ceremony, and his priests dance with the wad of cornstalks in the Corn dance.[1]

My efforts to discover the identity of the asperger who calls out the Keresan words, "*Tcamahía,*" etc,[2] at the *kisi,* have not been rewarded with great success. He apparently is not represented at Cipaulovi and Cuñopavi, but is personated at Oraibi and Walpi. He alone wears the coronet of cottonwood, and his body is characteristically decorated. Undoubtedly he is not one of the Antelope priests, for he takes no prominent part in Antelope secret rites. He is not a Snake priest in function or dress. Two facts throw a glimmer of light on his identity. The words which he calls out are Keresan words, and in the legend[3] of the Snake hero, "*Tcamahía*" is said to have left the Snake people and to have been joined by other clans at the Keresan pueblo, Acoma. In addition there may be quoted the statement of the Antelope chief that a personified representative from Acoma joins them biennially and assists them in the public exhibition of their dance. It seems as if the asperger who utters the Keresan invocation may personate a Keresan visitor, the ancestral wanderer, who left the Snake people in ancient times, and met other people from another direction at Acoma. His dress and speech are different, for he is not a Hopi; he is of the older stock, known by the same name as the ancient stone implements on the Antelope altar, *tcamahía,* the ancients, whom some of the Hopi claim did not come upon the earth through the same *sipapû* as themselves, but who at their advent were living in the far east.[4]

I have given much thought to the question why Antelope priests are so called, and what connection there can be between the antelope and the snake in this nomenclature. At one time I even doubted whether I could believe my Hopi friends in their statements that they were Antelope priests, notwithstanding their name, *Tcübwympkiya,* has the

---

[1] The erroneous statement that the "hugger" in the Snake dance is an Antelope priest is republished in many accounts of the Snake dance. This inaccuracy arose from the fact that in the Antelope dance an Antelope priest carried the wad of cornstalks and vines. Throughout the Snake dance all the Antelopes remain in line, singing, and holding such reptiles as are passed to them by the gatherers, but the "hugger" in the Snake dance is always a Snake priest.

[2] Journ. Amer. Eth. and Archæol., Vol. IV, pp. 73, 92.

[3] Op. cit., p. 117.

[4] With our present light it would be little more than plausible speculation to conclude that the Snake dances of the Rio Grande pueblos of Keresan stock originally came from Tusayan. That the Snake dance at Sia is closely alike that in Tusayan there is no doubt, and that Acoma had a Snake dance in 1583 is well known. A colony of Kawaika (Keresan) once lived in Antelope valley of Tusayan, or at least there is a ruin there called by the same name as Laguna, where there was also formerly a Snake dance. The indications are that the Keresan Snake dances are of the same source as those of the Hopi, but Keresan words in the Hopi invocation may admit of a different interpretation.

Antelope priests awaiting the Snake priests at the kisi

Preliminary circuit of the Snake priests in the Antelope dance

THE SNAKE DANCE AT ORAIBI

The dance before the reptiles are taken from the kisi

The snake carrier and the hugger

THE SNAKE DANCE AT ORAIBI

root of *tcübio*, antelope.[1] A study of the Oraibi altar effectually
silences all doubt on that score, for the effigies of antelopes' heads
form part of its paraphernalia. I have no satisfactory explanation of
the connection of the two priesthoods, but offer this suggestion: The
Ala or Horn people, now identified with the Flute, originally lived
with the Snake people, possibly as two phratries. When they separated, in an ancestral home, a majority wandered off with the Flute
people, but a few remained with the Snakes. The predominating clans
gave their names to the two groups, but although a number of the
Ala people remained with the Snakes, it was not large. These Ala
or Horn people were Antelopes, and their sacerdotal descendants are
the Antelope priests; but the clans were small and became extinct, and
the chiefs came from the predominating Snake family. The old name
of Antelope remained, and their symbol in effigy persists on the Oraibi
altar, but the clan was lost for a time.

Among the Flute branch the Ala people were vigorous, and retained
both blood and name, so that when Snake and Flute people came
together again, in Tusayan, they recognized each other as kin. At
that time, indeed, the Horn family existed in Walpi in Alosaka, and
he was naturally sent to spy out the character of the Flute men when
they came. This personage is still represented in the Flute dance at
that pueblo, as I have elsewhere described.[2]

Summing up the foregoing speculations, I am led to state the following probabilities which may be used as suggestions in future attempts
to divine the meaning of the Snake dance. That the ceremony is a
rain-making observance can not be doubted, and the nature of many
acts shows that it is likewise tinged with sun worship. To these must
now be added corn or seed germination, growth and maturity, implied
in the somewhat misleading name " Corn-dance," a dominating influence
in every great rite of Tusayan. I am inclined to believe that the Snake
dance has two main purposes, the making of rain and the growth of
corn, and renewed research confirms my belief, elsewhere expressed,
that ophiolatry has little or nothing to do with it. If there is any
worship of the snake, it is of such a nature that it may be more cor-
rectly designated ancestor worship. Nor does it appear to me that the
snake, as here used, is wholly a symbol of water, as the frog, tadpole,
or dragonfly. The reptile is introduced as a totemic personation by the
society of the Snake phratry to reproduce ancestral conditions in which
the ceremony was performed as the legend indicates. The same
thought is expressed in a similar way in widely different Tusayan ceremonies. Take any one of the *katcinas*, for instance; they do not introduce the totemic animal, to be sure, in the *Katcina* dance, but they
personate it by wearing masks. They thus attempt to resurrect the

---

[1] Note likewise the element *tcü* in *Tcüawympkiya*. Snake priest, and *Tcübwympkiya*, Antelope
priest.

[2] Journal of American Folk-lore, Vol. VII, No. xxvii, p. 287.

ancient performers or dramatize archaic celebrations. Where the drama induces them to introduce certain mythic animals, practical reasons lead them to personate what they can not obtain. They personate the duck (*Pawik*), and it is believed when they don the mask of *Pawik*, they become *Pawik katcinas,* and thus they perform the ceremony as did their totemic ancestors. Reptiles, however, are easy to obtain; their personation by men is therefore not necessary, and most tenacious of all in its influence, the presence of the snake is a startling component which fascinates and survives.

This theory implies but does not necessitate former belief in totemic descent. Certainly the evidence which we have leads us to believe that the Snake people, with a snake totem, believe they are descended from the Snake-woman, or if they stoutly deny descent from reptiles at present, may have once held it. Their denial, however, is only so much evidence, and is not necessarily decisive proof. White men as well as Indians deny many things which the comparative scientific method demonstrates to be true.

RESEMBLANCES TO THE KERESAN SNAKE DANCE

The valuable article by Mrs Stevenson gives us about all that is known of the character of the Snake dance among the Keres. Although Hodge[1] has found evidence that this ceremony was of late introduction in Sia, we may rightly suppose that the celebration described by Mrs Stevenson gives an idea of its general character among Keresan communities. I have already shown the points of similarity of the Snake dance of Walpi and that of Sia, as described by Mrs Stevenson, and have called attention to the probable meaning of those similarities, viz, derivation either from each other or differentiation of both from the same culture. The studies of the three Tusayan variants of the Snake dance, which are described in the preceding pages, add further evidence of relationship between the Tusayan and Keresan Snake dances. As would naturally be suspected, the Sia ceremonial differs more from any one Tusayan variant than the Tusayan dances differ among themselves, but the resemblances of the Oraibi, or most primitive, are closer to that of Sia than the highly differentiated Walpi performance.

The only other theory besides the derivation to account for these similarities of Tusayan and Keresan Snake dances would be that of independent origins, now being vigorously advocated in many quarters. While I am heartily in sympathy with this movement as a protest against wild comparisons and deductions from isolated likenesses of objects or myths, it may be carried too far. Members of the Keresan and Tusayan stocks, if we may so call them, have repeatedly been brought together in historic times. People from the Rio Grande have migrated in a body to Tusayan and built towns there or become assimilated with the sedentary inhabitants of that province. So, likewise, other peoples who once lived in Tusayan have moved back to the Rio Grande, and their descendants now form a component of pueblos like Laguna, Sandia, and others. This fact in itself is indicative of resemblances in ceremonials among these separated peoples, and when in studying the Snake dance of Sia and Tusayan we find many likenesses—not one or two resemblances in symbols and paraphernalia, but many resemblances in minute details—we rationally conclude that they are derivative and not of independent origins, due to a similar mind acted upon by a like environment.

---

[1] American Anthropologist, April, 1896, p. 134. Introduced by the "Cochiti somewhat more than thirty years ago."

The resemblances between Tusayan and Keresan Snake dances, which become more detailed as we study variants of the former at Oraibi and the Middle Mesa, render it less probable that two ceremonials coinciding in so many particulars originated independently. I hold, however, that we can not yet satisfactorily answer the question whether the Tusayan Snake dances were derived from the Keresan, or vice versa, or whether both differentiated from a common source.

Hodge[1] favors the idea that "the former Laguna Snake rites were introduced from the Hopi rather than from Acoma, where its influence was so slight as to leave not even a traditional trace," and he regards it quite likely that the Snake ceremony performed at Laguna only twenty years ago had its origin among the Hopi, and that it came, not "probably from Oraibi," as the Laguna people say, but more likely from the now ruined pueblo of Kawaika, whose name adhered to the newly founded pueblo near the lagoon. The people of the old "Kawaika" pueblo in Antelope valley came to Tusayan originally from the "far east," probably the Rio Grande. The theory that the Laguna Snake ceremony was derived from those Kawaikas who settled in Tusayan implies, of course, that some of them returned when Laguna was settled, which is possible; but the question whether the Acoma people did not have the Snake dance before western Kawaika was built, or before colonists left the east to settle in Antelope valley, is pertinent. If it had, as I suspect it did, the introduction of the Snake cult in Laguna from Tusayan pertains only to one Keresan locality, and we have yet to show that Acoma derived it from Tusayan. The Keresan songs and invocation in the Tusayan rites admit of but one interpretation. They at least were derived from Keresan sources.

The presentation of the Snake dance and accompanying Snake rites at Oraibi is closer to that of Sia than any of the Tusayan variants, and everything goes to show that it is the most primitive. The Walpi dance, on the other hand, has become more specialized, and is the most unlike the Sia as described by Mrs Stevenson;[2] but the question whether the Tusayan Snake cultus was derived from the Keresan, or vice versa, remains unanswered.

The meaning of the Snake dance can not, I believe, be made out completely without comparative studies, and can not be obtained from living priests. As pointed out by Tylor, in speaking of the religions of the great nations, so in that of Tusayan—

In the long and varied course in which religion has adapted itself to new intellectual and moral conditions, one of the most marked processes has affected time-honored religious customs, whose form has been faithfully and even servilely kept up while their nature has often undergone transformation. . . . The natural difficulty of following these changes has been added to by the sacerdotal tendency to ignore and obliterate traces of the inevitable change of religion from age to age, and to convert into mysteries ancient rites whose real barbaric meaning is too far out of harmony with the spirit of a later time.[3]

---

[1] Op. cit., p. 135.
[2] Eleventh Annual Report of the Bureau of Ethnology.
[3] Primitive Culture, Vol. II, p. 363.

I have no doubt that at some future time enough material will be collected to enable the ethnologist to give a rational explanation of the meaning of the Snake dance from comparative studies, but I doubt very much whether the Tusayan priests now know its original meaning. The trail for the ethnographer is, however, plain; it is highly essential that renewed efforts be made to record more accurately than has yet been done the unknown details of the Tusayan Snake dance before it is finally abandoned or transformed by modifications. Whatever current explanations are now regarded as orthodox by the priests should be given weight as evidence, but not regarded as decisive.

Of more than usual interest in a study of the distribution of the Snake ceremonials is the following reference, which I quote without comment:

It was discovered [that] the Cocopahs, like the Moquis of Arizona, practice the Snake Dance ceremony. Not far from their village is an old adobe house especially constructed for this purpose. Here they annually resort, to avoid publicity, to have their Snake dance. Rattlesnakes are taken to this house, where the people of the Snake clan congregate and perform their hazardous ceremony. (From letter in *Chicago Tribune*, dated Pomona, Cal., October 31, 1895?)

BIBLIOGRAPHY[1]

BAXTER, RUPERT H. The Moqui Snake Dance.

American Antiquarian, Vol. XVII, No. 4, Good Hope, Ill., July, 1895.

BOURKE, JOHN G. The Snake Ceremonials at Walpi.

American Anthropologist, Washington, April, 1895.

COE, CURTIS P. Moqui Snake Dance.

Moqui Mission Messenger, Vol. I, Nos. 8, 9.

FEWKES, J. WALTER. The Oraibi Flute Altar.

Journal of American Folk-lore, Vol. VIII, No. 31, Boston, October-December, 1895. (Notes on Walpi Snake dance of 1895.)

—— A Comparison of Sia and Tusayan Snake Ceremonials.

American Anthropologist, Vol. VIII, No. 2, Washington, April, 1895.

GARLAND, HAMLIN. Among the Moqui Indians.

Harper's Weekly, August 15, 1896, illustrated by Lungren. (The best popular account of the Walpi Snake dance yet published.)

HODGE, F. W. Pueblo Snake Ceremonials.

American Anthropologist, Vol. IX, No. 4, April, 1896.

MASILLON, C. Les Indiens Moki et leur danse de serpent.

Nature, Vol. XXIV, Paris, 1896.

POLITZER, J. H. Snake Dance of the Moquis.

Herald, New York, November 11, 1894.

—— Mouthfuls of Rattlesnakes.

Examiner, San Francisco, October 21, 1894.

—— The Moqui Serpent Dance.

Republic, St. Louis, November 7, 1894.

—— Among the Moquis.

Daily Traveller, Boston, November 7, 1894. (Describes Oraibi Snake dance.)

RUST, H. N. The Moqui Snake Dance.

Land of Sunshine, Los Angeles, January. 1896. (Illustrated account of Walpi Snake Dance of 1895.)

—— Through Arizona's Wonderland.

Inter Ocean, Chicago, July 26, 1896.

STEVENSON, M. C. The Sia.

Eleventh Annual Report of the Bureau of Ethnology, Washington, 1894. (Contains a description of the snake ceremonies of Sia pueblo.)

ANONYMOUS. Snake Dance of the Moqui Indians; a religious drama and a prayer for rain.

Times-Herald, Chicago, October 13, 1895.

—— The Snake Dance.

Journal, Boston, August 28, 1895.

—— A Moqui Snake Dance.

Bulletin, San Francisco, September 3, 1895: Evening Sun, New York, September 14, 1895.

—— Snake Dance of the Moquis.

Herald, New York, November 11, 1894; Bee, Omaha, September 22, 1895.

—— An Indian Snake Dance.

Register, New Haven, September 22, 1895.

—— Weird Arizona Snake Dance.

Evening Gazette, Boston, October 10, 1896, reprinted from the World, New York.

—— Amid Ancient Moqui Ruins. The Famous Snake Dance.

Times, Washington, September 28, 1896.

—— With the Snake Dancers.

Call, San Francisco, January 31, 1896.

—— Moqui Snake Dances.

Scimitar, Memphis, October 21, 1896.

—— The Moqui Snake Dances.

Sun, New York, October 4, 1896.

—— Hideous Rites.

Globe, Utica, October 10, 1896.

[1] From the varied and scattered newspapers and magazines in which accounts of the Snake dance have been published and copied, it is almost impossible to make this bibliography complete. Reviews of works on the Snake dance, of which I have over thirty, are not mentioned.

The author has not completed his studies on the Snake dance, and would be glad to communicate with other students on this subject. The more important articles on the Walpi Snake dance of 1891 and 1893 are mentioned in the Journal of American Ethnology and Archæology, Vol. IV.

The Oraibi performance

The Cipaulovi performance

SNAKE PRIESTS WITH REPTILES

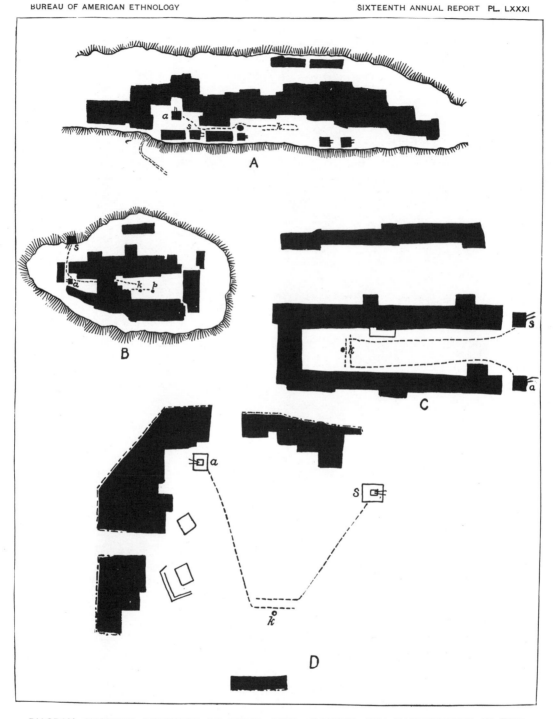

DIAGRAM SHOWING POSITIONS OF KIVAS, KISIS, SHRINES, AND PARTICIPANTS IN THE
SNAKE CEREMONIALS

a, Walpi   *b*, Cipaulovi   *c*, Cuñopavi   *d*, Oraibi

SNAKE DANCE, HOPI, ARIZONA, COURTESY OF THE MUSEUM OF NEW MEXICO, NEG. NO. 146658

PHOTOGRAPHER AND DATE UNKNOWN, WALPI VILLAGE,
COURTESY SPECIAL COLLECTIONS, ZIMMERMAN LIBRARY,
UNIVERSITY OF NEW MEXICO

BEN WITTICK, AUGUST 17, 1889, WALPI VILLAGE,
COURTESY MUSEUM OF NEW MEXICO NEG. NO. 16077

PHOTOGRAPHER, DATE AND VILLAGE UNKNOWN, COURTESY
MUSEUM OF NEW MEXICO NEG. NO. 108307

HOPI "SNAKE DANCE"

PHOTOGRAPHER DATE AND VILLAGE UNKNOWN, COURTESY
MUSEUM OF NEW MEXICO NEG. NO. 74745

BEN WITTICK, AUGUST 19, 1897, MISHONGNOVI VILLAGE,
COURTESY MUSEUM OF NEW MEXICO NEG. NO. 102068

H.F. ROBINSON, CIRCA 1910 VIILAGE UNKNOWN, COURTESY
SPECIAL COLLECTIONS, ZIMMERMAN LIBRARY, UNIVERSITY
OF NEW MEXICO

H.F. ROBINSON, CIRCA 1910, VILLAGE UNKNOWN, COURTESY
OF MUSEUM OF NEW MEXICO NEG. NO. 37381

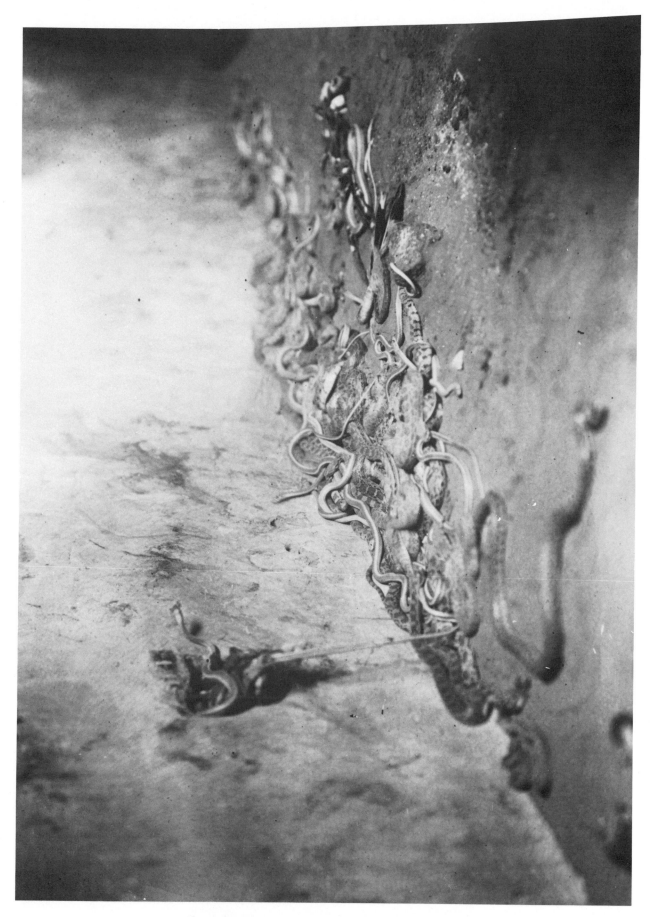

GEORGE WHARTON JAMES, AUGUST, 1897, WALPI VILLAGE,
"THE SNAKES AFTER THE WASHING CEREMONIES IN THE KIVA",
COURTESY MUSEUM OF NEW MEXICO NEG. NO. 14436

PHOTOGRAPHER AND DATE UNKNOWN, WALPI VILLAGE,
COURTESY SPECIAL COLLECTIONS, ZIMMERMAN LIBRARY,
UNIVERSITY OF NEW MEXICO

HOPI SNAKE DANCE, HOPI, ARIZONA, COURTESY OF THE MUSEUM OF NEW MEXICO NEG. NO. 134951

SNAKES, SNAKE DANCE, HOPI, ARIZONA, CA 1913, PHOTO PROBABLY BY H.F. ROBINSON, COURTESY OF THE MUSEUM OF NEW MEXICO NEG. NO. 21603

NINETEENTH ANNUAL REPORT

OF THE

BUREAU OF AMERICAN ETHNOLOGY

TO THE

SECRETARY OF THE SMITHSONIAN INSTITUTION

1897-98

BY

J. W. POWELL

DIRECTOR

IN TWO PARTS—PART 2

WASHINGTON
GOVERNMENT PRINTING OFFICE
1900

TUSAYAN FLUTE AND SNAKE CEREMONIES

BY

JESSE WALTER FEWKES

CONTENTS

ILLUSTRATIONS

961

SNAKE DANCE AT MISHONGNOVI

M. Wright Gill

A. HOEN & CO. LITHOCAUSTIC, BALTIMORE.

NOTES ON TUSAYAN, SNAKE, AND FLUTE CEREMONIES

By Jesse Walter Fewkes

INTRODUCTION

The Hopi or so-called Moqui Indians of Arizona are among the few surviving tribes of American aborigines which still retain an ancient ritual that is apparently unmodified by the Christian religion. This ritual is of a very complicated nature and is composed of monthly ceremonies the recurrence of which is precise as to time and place.

It must be remembered that these ceremonies are not performed at irregular intervals by well-to-do Hopi to cure sickness of themselves or their families. Among other Indians this motive is often the keynote of their rites, but while among the Hopi there are ceremonials which are directed to that end, and all the regularly recurring ceremonials are regarded as efficacious in healing bodily ills, they have primarily another purpose. Whether they originated as a preventive of disease, and in their primitive condition had the same intent as the rites of the Navaho shamans, is beyond the scope of this memoir. At present the ritual is performed for the purpose of bringing abundant rains and successful crops.

Two most important summer ceremonies in this elaborate ritual are the Snake dance and the Flute observance, and the former, from the startling fact that venomous reptiles are carried in the mouths of the participants, has achieved world-wide celebrity. It is thought by some white men to be the most important ceremony in the calendar, but anyone familiar with the Hopi ritual will recognize that these Indians have several other ceremonies more complicated, though far less sensational. Only the bare outlines of many of these ceremonies have yet been described, but enough is known to cause due appreciation of their importance in the Hopi system of religion. The Flute ceremony is one of these, and as it is closely connected with the Snake dance it is naturally considered in this connection.

With the accompanying description of the Snake dance at Mishongnovi the author completes his account of the general features of this ceremony in the five Tusayan pueblos in which it takes place, but this additional knowledge of the externals of the observance has by

963

no means exhausted the subject, as the translation of songs and prayers is yet to be made.

The existence of a Snake dance among the Hopi villages was called to the attention of ethnologists about fifteen years ago, and in late years it has been repeatedly witnessed and described in detail by many observers, but it is hoped that the additional light thrown on the subject by the present studies may further advance our knowledge and prove an aid to more important discoveries.

The present paper has been prepared from notes made at the Hopi pueblos in the summers of 1896 and 1897. At the time these studies were made the author was in charge of an archæologic expedition sent out by the Bureau of American Ethnology, and could give but little of his time to ethnologic investigations. It was impossible to follow the complicated secret rites of the ceremonies through their entire course, consequently this account is limited to those portions which are most obscure. The author studied with care the Snake dance at Mishongnovi and the Flute observance in the same pueblo, of which little was known save the altars. Studies of the latter were conducted in 1896 and of the former in 1897. Certain comparisons with the Walpi Flute ceremony, and new data obtained in 1896, are likewise introduced.

SNAKE DANCE AT MISHONGNOVI IN 1897

A detailed preliminary account of the Snake dance at Walpi in 1891 and 1893 has been given elsewhere,[1] and the general features of that at Shipaulovi, Shumopovi, and Oraibi, as observed in 1896, are also recorded in a previous publication.[2]

The Snake dance covers a period of at least sixteen days, nine of which are days of active ceremonies, secret or open. These nine days bear the following names: 1, Yuñya; 2, Custala; 3, Luctala; 4, Paictala; 5, Naluctala; 6, Sockahimû; 7, Komoktotokya; 8, Totokya;[3] 9, Tihuni.[3]

The author arrived at Mishongnovi on August 16 of the year named, on Totokya, the day preceding that on which the final dance occurred, and saw the public Antelope ceremony performed. He likewise witnessed the Snake race on the morning of the ninth day (Tihuni), and studied the altar of the Antelope priests, and certain of their sacred rites. The only kiva rite of the Snake priests which was witnessed was the snake washing on the afternoon of the last day.[4]

---

[1] Journal of American Ethnology and Archæology, vol. IV.

[2] Sixteenth Annual Report of the Bureau of American Ethnology.

[3] The author was present at Mishongnovi on these days.

[4] Other members of the party were Dr Walter Hough, of the National Museum, and Mr F. W. Hodge, of the Bureau of American Ethnology. It was found convenient to camp at the small spring to the east of the Middle mesa on the trail to Walpi. As this spring can be readily approached by wagons it is recommended as a suitable place for visitors who do not desire to remain in the pueblos overnight.

This article is a record only of what was seen, and lays no claim to completeness, introducing no rites which were not studied, even when there is ample proof of their existence (and the same may be said of the previously cited accounts of the Snake dances at Oraibi and the Middle mesa). Like the preceding accounts, it is simply a preliminary record to aid investigators in future studies until enough material has been accumulated to adequately fathom the meaning of the rites.

The portions of the Snake ceremony to which special attention was given were the altars, the washing of the reptiles, and the public Antelope and Snake dances. There still remain to be investigated several important episodes, such as the rites and songs about the altar. It is expected that this and other fragmentary contributions to the subject will lead to an exhaustive account of the Hopi Snake dance, which the author has had in preparation for the last eight years.

The only known description of the Snake dance at Mishongnovi (plate XLV) was published in Science in 1886, by Mr Cosmos Mindeleff, who witnessed the festival at the pueblo named on August 16, 1885, and saw the presentation at Walpi on the following day. He found the two performances "essentially the same, the only difference being in the greater number of performers at Walpi, and in the painting of the body." In a general way this is true, but there are important differences in the kiva paraphernalia and performances, which are characteristic and instructive in comparative studies of the dance. Mr Mindeleff noticed the sand altar, and gave a brief description of it without illustration. He confused the two kivas used, for he speaks of a sand altar in the "Snake kiva proper," or "easternmost kiva." The room where the Snake priests meet and where the reptiles are confined has no altar, which in Mishongnovi is always made in a neighboring room, the Antelope kiva. While observations on the public dance agree with Mindeleff's descriptions, there are significant differences in interpretation, due to enlarged acquaintance with the Hopi ritual. "The Snake gens," he writes, "has nothing to do with the dance, and contrary to the opinion of Captain Bourke it is not referable, I think, to ancestor worship, at least not directly." On the contrary, no one can now doubt that the Snake dance was primarily a part of the ritual of the Snake clan, and that ancestor worship is very prominent in it. We need only look to the clan relation of the majority of priests in the celebration to show its intimate connection with the Snake clan, for the Snake chief, the Antelope chief, and all the adult men of the Snake family participate in it. The reverence with which the ancestor, and particularly the ancestress, of the Snake clan, viz, Tcüamana, is regarded, and the personation of these beings in kiva rites, certainly gives strong support to a theory of totemistic ancestor worship.

The reptiles used in the dance are collected on four successive days; the Antelope and Snake races, as well as several other episodes of the Mishongnovi ceremonial, are known to conform essentially to those at Walpi, before described.

The Mishongnovi Antelope Altar

The two kivas at Mishongnovi occupied by the Antelope and Snake societies lie not far apart, on the side of the village facing west. The one to the left, as one looks at them from the housetops, was occupied by the Snake priests; that to the right by the Antelope priests. Like all Tusayan kivas, these chambers are separated from the houses, and are rectangular in shape. They are subterranean, with an interior arrangement quite like those of Walpi. The Antelope and the Snake kivas are the only ones in Mishongnovi which the author visited, but Mr Victor Mindeleff mentions the names of five, and Mr Cosmos Mindeleff speaks of three. Evidently, if these enumerations be correct, some of the chambers have been abandoned within a recent period.

The Antelope altar at Mishongnovi (plate XLVI) resembles that at Walpi,[1] Oraibi, Shipaulovi, and Shumopovi[2] in its essential features, but there are differences in detail. There was no altar in the kiva used by the Snake priests in this pueblo, and this was also true in the other Hopi pueblos, except Walpi. The dual wooden images of Püükoñ and the female counterpart in the Oraibi[3] Snake kiva are not in themselves an indication of an altar; for the essential object in a Snake altar is the Snake palladium, or tiponi, which does not exist in this pueblo, and, indeed, is found only at Walpi.

The number of tiponis, or chieftain's badges, which are placed on the altars of the Antelope priests varies in the Hopi pueblos. Walpi and Oraibi have two; Shipaulovi and Shumopovi, one each. There are two tiponis on the Antelope altar at Mishongnovi, both of which are carried by Antelope chiefs in the public dances. Neither of these corresponds with the Snake tiponi of the Walpi chief, who has the only known Snake tiponi. The position of the two tiponis on the altar is characteristic, for they stand one on each of the rear corners of the sand picture, and not midway in the length of the rear margin, as at Oraibi and Walpi.

The sand picture of the Antelope altar at Mishongnovi resembles that of the other Antelope societies. Its border is composed of four bands of differently colored sand—yellow, green, red, and white—arranged in the order given from within outward. These marginal bands correspond with the cardinal points and are separated

---

[1] Snake ceremonials at Walpi, Journ. Amer. Eth. and Arch., vol. IV.

[2] Tusayan Snake ceremonies, Sixteenth Annual Report of the Bureau of American Ethnology.

[3] On certain years an altar is said to be introduced in initiations.

ANTELOPE ALTAR AT MISHONGNOVI

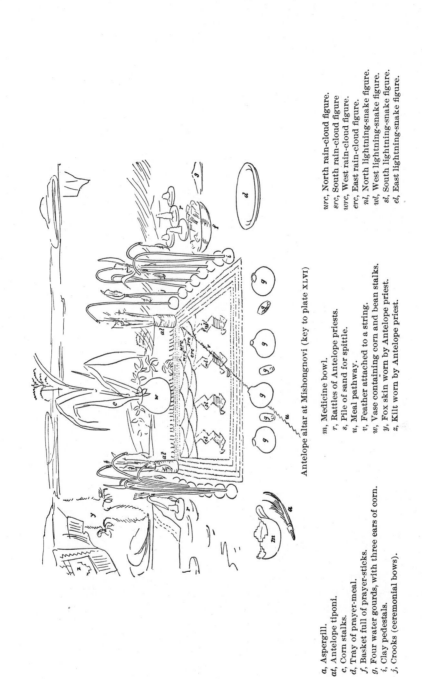

Antelope altar at Mishongnovi (key to plate XLVI)

a, Aspergill.
at, Antelope tiponi.
c, Corn stalks.
d, Tray of prayer-meal.
f, Basket full of prayer-sticks.
g, Four water gourds, with three ears of corn.
i, Clay pedestals.
j, Crooks (ceremonial bows).

m, Medicine bowl.
r, Rattles of Antelope priests.
s, Pile of sand for spittle.
u, Meal pathway.
v, Feather attached to a string.
w, Vase containing corn and bean stalks.
y, Fox skin worn by Antelope priest.
z, Kilt worn by Antelope priest.

nrc, North rain-cloud figure.
src, South rain-cloud figure
wrc, West rain-cloud figure.
erc, East rain-cloud figure.
nl, North lightning-snake figure.
wl, West lightning-snake figure.
sl, South lightning-snake figure.
el, East lightning-snake figure.

by black lines. In the inclosed field, which is white, there are four sets of semicircles of the same colors, each with four members also separated by black lines, and on the border there are a number of short parallel lines. These semicircles represent rain-clouds, and the parallel lines, falling rain.

The semicircular figures occupy about one-third of the inclosed field, and in the remainder there are four zigzag designs representing lightning, as snakes, colored yellow, green, red, and white, with black rims. Each lightning symbol has a triangular head, with two dots for eyes and parallel marks for a necklace. Appended to the head of each is a horn.

On each side of the sand picture a row of sticks are set upright in clay pedestals. These sticks, like those at Oraibi, are straight, and not crooked at the end, as at Walpi. On the last day of the ceremony it is customary for the Antelope priests to hang the bundles of feathers which they wear on their heads on these sticks, as is shown in the picture of the Walpi altar (plate LIII). The straight sticks probably represent arrows, and possibly, when curved at the end, primitive implements of war, allied to bows, for the propulsion of arrow-like weapons.[1]

Back of the sand painting, about midway in the length of the rear margin, and slightly removed from it, was a small vase containing cornstalks and gourd vines. This vase is called a "patne" and corresponds with that which the Snake-girl at Walpi holds in her hand during the dramatizations of the Snake legend, elsewhere described. Unfortunately there is nothing known of the part this vase plays in the secret exercises in any pueblo but Walpi; yet it probably has a similar rôle in all. It may be said, in passing, that a similar vase is found on all Antelope altars, even the simplest; and there is no known Antelope altar where cornstalks and vines are absent on the last days of the ceremony.

Four spherical netted gourds were placed at equal intervals along the front margin of the sand picture. These gourds, which were later carried by the Antelope priests in the public dance, are represented at Oraibi by a row of similar objects on each side of the altar. Between each pair of these gourds there was an ear of corn, as is shown in the plate. The author's studies have not proceeded far enough to enable him to connect these ears of corn with those of novices, which,

---

[1] The author's illustration of the Oraibi altar is faulty in representing these sticks crooked at the end. They are straight in this pueblo as well as at Shipaulovi, as was stated in the descriptive text in the Sixteenth Annual Report of the Bureau of American Ethnology, p. 279. In the Oraibi Snake (not Antelope) dance the priests do not carry these rods from the altar. The left hands of all, with the exception of the man who carried an ear of corn, of the chief, who had his tiponi, and of the asperger, who bore the medicine-bowl and aspergill, were empty. Thirteen of the sticks were counted on the left side of the altar, and there were probably an equal number on the right side. There were no stone images of animals on this altar, and the stone "tcamahias" which are so conspicuous in the Walpi altar between the clay pedestals and the border of the sand picture were likewise absent. There were no sticks along the front of the sand picture as at Walpi, where, by their distribution, spaces or gateways are left in the altar.

ENTRANCE TO MISHONGNOVI SNAKE KIVA

PLATOON OF ANTELOPE PRIESTS AT MISHONGNOVI

at Walpi, are generally placed on a basket tray near the altar. It is possible that they belong to novices, but their fate when the altar was destroyed was not noticed. Four netted gourds were carried by the Antelope priests in the public dance.

In the public dance at Oraibi each Antelope priest carried one of these water gourds, while in the other pueblos, where the number of participants is smaller, only one or two priests bear these objects. At Walpi, for instance, the Antelope chief has one of the water gourds which is not conspicuous in the public ceremony. At the Middle mesa several gourds are used, while at Oraibi they form an important feature of the ceremonial paraphernalia, and it is probable that the conditions at Oraibi are nearer the ancient than at Walpi in this particular. A number of basket trays containing prayer-sticks occupied the whole space of the floor between the altar and the fireplace. This is similar to what is found at Shipaulovi, as shown in a figure of the altar of that pueblo.[1]

There is good evidence that the Walpi custom of making prayer-sticks of different lengths, corresponding to the length of finger joints, and of prescribing the days of their manufacture and the distance of the shrines in which they are deposited, is not followed at Shipaulovi, Oraibi, and Mishongnovi.

While there is a general similarity between the pahos made by the Antelope societies in all the Tusayan pueblos, there are differences in detail. One of the component sticks is provided with a flat facet, on which is painted eyes and mouth, forming a rude representation of a face. While this facet is absent from the Walpi Snake and Antelope pahos, the two sticks which compose the prayer-offering are regarded as male and female.

SNAKE WHIPS

On entering the Mishongnovi Snake kiva all the snake whips were found to be arranged in a row against a banquette at the end of the room. A similar arrangement has also been noticed in the Snake kiva at Shipaulovi, but there was no evidence of an altar or sand picture in the Snake chamber in either of the pueblos named. The snake whips are composed of two shafts, instead of one, with a corn-husk packet of meal tied about the middle. This would seem to indicate that the whips were regarded as prayer-sticks, and indeed this name (paho) is applied to them. During the ceremony of washing the reptiles a small ''breath feather'' of the eagle, stained red, is tied to the scalplock, but later this feather is detached and fastened by one of the priests to the end of his whip.

---

[1] Sixteenth Annual Report of the Bureau of American Ethnology, plate LXXI.

SNAKE-HUNTING IMPLEMENTS

It is customary for the Snake priests on the four snake hunts to dig out the reptiles from their holes with sticks and hoes. These implements are left on the kiva roof overnight, or while the priests are in the pueblos, and must not be carried to the homes of the owners until the close of the dance. There were noted at Mishongnovi many Hopi planting sticks, a number of American hoes, several old Mexican mattocks, and flat iron knives, also of Mexican manufacture, tied to sticks. At Walpi, Mexican implements have almost wholly passed out of use, but in the Middle mesa villages and at Oraibi they are still employed. The Snake chief would not part with one of these hoes during the ceremony, but had no objection to selling one or more of them after the festival.

WASHING THE REPTILES

One of the weirdest of the many features of the Snake ceremony in the Hopi pueblos is the washing of the reptiles used by the priests. This occurs in all the villages just after noon of the ninth day, and is preparatory to bringing the snakes to the public plaza, from which they are later taken and carried by members of the Snake society in the presence of spectators. The details of this rite, as performed at Walpi, have been described, but no one has yet recorded the variants of snake washing in the other four Hopi villages where it is celebrated.

In order to gather information in regard to snake washing in the other pueblos, the author attended the performance of this rite at Mishongnovi on August 17, 1897. The snake washing at Oraibi and on the Middle mesa pueblos is greatly modified by the absence of a sand altar such as exists at Walpi. In considering the reason for the absence of the Snake altars in these villages, a corresponding absence of a Snake tiponi or badge of chieftaincy is to be noted. Walpi, on the East mesa, is the only Hopi village that has a Snake tiponi.

Considerable time was spent before the snake washing began in getting the reptiles out of the four canteens in which they were kept when not moving about freely in the kiva. These canteens are of baked clay similar to those in which the women carry water on their backs to the pueblos from the springs at the base of the mesa. A hole is punched in the middle of the convex side, and both this and the opening at the neck are closed with corncobs. The reptiles were transferred with difficulty from these vessels to cloth bags, and were laid on the floor near the fireplace. A considerable quantity of sand was brought into the room and spread on the floor on one side of the kiva. A board was placed on a stone seat along the edge of this sand, down the middle of the kiva, and upon this board the Snake priests seated themselves, facing the sanded floor. They were closely

THE KALEKTAKA AT WALPI

WIKI, ANTELOPE CHIEF

crowded together, completely surrounding the sand, save on one side, which was formed by the kiva wall (see figure 42). Three boys— novices—stood behind the line of seated priests, and if any of the rep- tiles escaped between the men while being released, they were promptly captured and returned to the sand by the lads.

The bodies of all the participants were naked and were stained red with iron oxide, and each man wore a small red feather in his hair. Before taking their seats they hung bandoliers over their shoulders and tied one to the ladder pole. One of their number tied a white buckskin over his arm, and added other paraphernalia characteristic

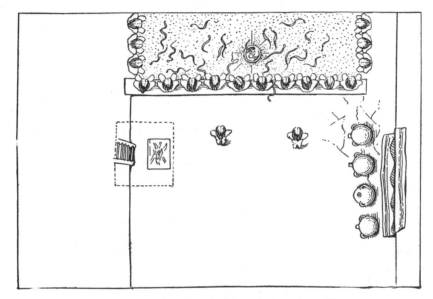

Fig. 42—Diagram of positions of celebrants in the snake washing.

of a kalektaka or warrior. It may be here noted that this personifi- cation does not appear in the Walpi snake washing.

Two Snake kilts were spread on the banquette at the end of the kiva, and leaning against one of these was a row of snake whips. One of these kilts was decorated with a complete figure of the Great Snake. Ordinarily the head is omitted from figures of this serpent on Snake kilts, but the Snake priest at the Keres pueblo of Sia, as repre- sented in Mrs Stevenson's instructive memoir, wears a kilt decorated with a complete figure of the Great Serpent. The figure of the zigzag body of the Great Snake on the kilts at the Middle mesa and Oraibi has two parallel bars extending entirely across the design; in the Snake kilts used in Walpi these lines do not join the border, but are parallel with it.

The chief sat in the middle of the line and a man dressed as a war- rior was at his side. The former first drew with meal on the sand before him six short radiating lines corresponding to the six cardinal points recognized by the Hopi, and at their junction he placed a large earthenware basin similar to the kind used in washing the head. Into this bowl the chief poured liquid from a large gourd six times, each time making a pass in sequence to one of the cardinal directions. The remaining liquid was then emptied into the bowl so that it was about two-thirds full. Some object, an herb or root, which was not plainly seen, was next put into the liquid.

A formal ceremonial smoke followed, during which terms of relationship were interchanged among the men. When this had ceased prayers were offered by several of the priests, beginning with the Snake chief. The Snake men then took their snake whips and began a quick song resembling that of the Walpi society during a similar rite, and the priests took the reptiles from the bags and transferred them, three or four at a time, to the liquid. They were then laid on the sand, but were not thrown across the room, as at the Walpi snake washing. The object of placing the reptiles on the sand was simply to dry them, and they were left there for some time after their transference from the bowl of liquid. At the close of the rite the priests resumed the preparation of their dance paraphernalia, painting their kilts, and decorating their bandoliers with the shells which had been given them by the author.

The participants, even when the reptiles were free in the kiva, were not restrained by many of the prescribed rules of conduct which are so rigidly adhered to at Walpi. Members of the society did not lower their voices in conversation, and even loud talking was engaged in during the snake washing. No one at that time speaks above a whisper in the Walpi kiva, and loud conversation is never heard.

The wearing of their bandoliers by the Snake priests during the snake washing seems to be a survival of a primitive custom that has disappeared at Walpi, and the personation of a warrior by one of their number may have a similar explanation. It is interesting in this connection to note that in the Walpi celebration a similar warrior personator accompanies the Antelope priests, among whom he is conspicuous, but he does not appear associated with them in variants of the Snake dances which have been studied in other Hopi pueblos. In the Walpi snake washing, when the Snake chief deposits on the sand the bowl in which the reptiles are washed, he makes four raincloud symbols. At Mishongnovi the chief simply draws six radiating lines of meal, but it would seem that the intent was the same in both instances, the Middle mesa practice being perhaps more ancient. At Mishongnovi it was not noticed whether a bandolier[1] was placed under the basin in which the snakes were washed, as is the case at Walpi.

---

[1] Many of the bandoliers were decorated with rows of small cones, the spines of shells identical with specimens which are occasionally dug from ruins along Little Colorado river. The conus shell, from which these are made, is found in ruins along the Gila, and was used as an ornament, or, fastened with others to a stick, served as a rattle to beat time in rhythm with sacred songs.

The idea which underlies the washing of the reptiles in the Snake dance is that of bodily purification or lustration, and probably sprang from a belief in a totemic relationship between reptiles and the Snake clan. It can be explained on the theory that the reptiles, as "elder brothers" and members of the same Snake clan, need purification by water as an essential act in preparation for the ceremonials in which they later participate.

On the morning of the ninth day of the Snake dance all priests of the Snake society and all members of the Snake clan bathe their heads in preparation for the ceremony. The reptiles, or elder members of the same clan, have been gathered from the fields and brought to the pueblo to participate in this the great festival of their family, and it is both fitting and necessary that their heads, like those of the priests, should be washed on this day. The ceremonial washing of the reptiles is therefore perfectly logical on the theory of totemic worship.

A few days after the snake washing at Mishongnovi, the author attended for the fourth time the snake washing at Walpi, finding that the rites presented no marked variation from those of previous years. The exercises at the Middle mesa, and probably at Oraibi, lack the dash of those of the East mesa, and are simpler in character.

The Snake priests of Walpi found it necessary to station one of their number at the hatchway, as a tyler, to prevent the intrusion of the uninitiated during the snake washing, and this will probably become a custom in future dances.

Public Antelope and Snake Dances

The public Snake dance at Mishongnovi (plate XLV) has been well described by Mr Cosmos Mindeleff.[1] It closely resembles that at Walpi, which it generally precedes,[2] and, next to that at Walpi, it is the most spirited performance of this ceremony 'among the Hopi. On account of their similarity it is hardly necessary to describe both the Antelope and the Snake dance, and consequently this account is limited to the latter, or to details in which differences exist.

A conical structure made of cottonwood boughs, and called a kisi (brush-house), was erected in the plaza near a central, permanent shrine of stone. The kisi served as a receptacle for the reptiles until they were needed, and was made in the following way: holes were dug in the ground at intervals in the form of a circle, and several good size, newly cut but untrimmed, green cottonwood boughs were planted therein. The upper ends of the boughs were bound together with ropes and straps, and a cloth was tied on one side covering an entrance into the inclosure. Smaller cottonwood branches were inserted between the larger ones, making a dense bower amply suffi-

---

[1] Science, vol. VII, number 174, 1886.

[2] In 1891, 1893, and 1895 it was celebrated the day before the Walpi dance, and in 1885, according to Mindeleff, the same relative day was chosen.

cient to conceal whatever was placed within. Shortly before the dance began a sack containing all the reptiles was deposited in the kisi by two Snake priests.

The public ceremony was ushered in by the appearance of the line of Antelope priests, headed by their chief, who carried his tiponi on his left arm. There were twenty persons in this procession, the rear of which consisted of four small boys. Next to the chief came an albino, likewise bearing a tiponi on his arm. The Antelope priests were dressed and painted as are those of Walpi, but the four small boys who closed the line wore very small kilts. In the 1885 celebration, according to Mindeleff, there were but ten Antelope priests in line. The increase in number is in accord with what has been observed at Walpi, where the number of participants has also increased in late years.

Each Antelope priest, except one to be presently noticed, carried two rattles, one in each hand, which is characteristic of two of the Middle mesa pueblos, but different from the custom at Walpi and Oraibi, where each Antelope priest carries one rattle only.

The third man in the line bore a medicine-bowl and an aspergill; he wore a fillet of cottonwood leaves, and was comparable with the asperger of the Walpi and other variants. He dipped his feathered aspergill into the medicine-bowl as he entered and left the plaza, and asperged to world-quarters and upon the Snake priests. Before the snake dance began, this man called out an invocation to warriors.

In an account of the Oraibi dance it has been noted that the words of this invocation, which have long been recognized as foreign to the Hopi language, were also used in Keresan songs at Sia pueblo. In the course of these new investigations direct inquiries were made in regard to the meaning of the words, and the identity of the personation by the man who utters them. The man who makes this invocation is believed to represent the Acoma relatives of the Snake people. There are several songs in Hopi secret rites, the words of which resemble closely certain terms of the Keresan language, in addition to the vocables common to sacred songs of all American Indians.

The line of Antelope priests made four circuits about the plaza, and as each member passed the shrine in the middle of the plaza, he dropped a pinch of meal upon it. The same act of prayer was repeated before the kisi when the priest stamped violently on a plank as he dropped the sacred meal. The Antelopes then formed a platoon at the kisi and awaited the Snake priests, who soon appeared, headed by the Snake chief.

When the Antelope priests had formed in a platoon in front of the kisi (plate XVLIII), it was noticed that the line was continuous and not broken into two divisions, a right and a left, as at Walpi. The first four men and the ninth man in line, counting from the left, were barefoot, but all the remainder wore moccasins. There was some variation in the colors of the feathers on their heads, which can be interpreted in the same way as similar variations at Walpi, later considered; but it was noticed that certain of the priests failed to have the white zigzag markings on their bodies, so conspicuous in the Walpi celebration.

The entrance of the Snake priests into the plaza was not so animated as at Walpi under the leadership of Kopeli, but their circuits were the same, and their dress and adornment was quite similar in the two pueblos. The Snake priests filed about the plaza four times, stamped on the plank in the ground before the kisi as they passed it, and took their positions facing the Antelope priests. The ceremonies at the kisi began with a swaying movement of their bodies in unison with the song of the Antelopes, and, as it continued, the Snake priests locked arms, and, bending over, shook their whips at the ground with a quivering motion as if brushing a vicious snake from a coiled posture. These preliminary songs, with attendant steps, lasted about a quarter of an hour, at the close of which time the startling feature of the ceremony—the carrying of the reptiles about the plaza—began. This was one of the best presentations of the Snake dance ever seen in the Hopi pueblos.

One of the most conspicuous men in the line of Snake priests personified a warrior (kalektaka), who wore on his head a close-fitting, open-mesh, cotton skull-cap, which represents the ancient war-bonnet.[1] This warrior-personation entered the kisi, and there, concealed from view, held the neck of the bag in which the reptiles were confined to the entrance of the kisi, and as the imprisoned snakes were needed he drew or forced them from the bag to be taken by those outside.

The Snake priests divided into groups of three, each group consisting of a "carrier" who held the reptile in his mouth, a "hugger" who placed his left hand on the right shoulder of the carrier, whom he accompanied in his circuit about the plaza, and the "gatherer," who collected and carried the snakes after they were dropped. The reptiles were not handed to the Antelope priests to hold during the dance. As the priests circled about with the snakes in their mouths, two platoons of women sprinkled them with sacred meal from trays which they held as a prayer-offering. The Antelopes remained in line by the kisi, singing and shaking their rattles as the rite progressed.

At the close of the dance the chief made a ring of meal on the ground, in which he drew six radial lines corresponding to the cardinal points, and all the reptiles were placed within this circle. At a signal after a prayer the Snake priests rushed at the struggling mass, and seizing

---

[1] The wooden image, in the Oraibi Snake kiva, representing Püükoñ, has on its head the representation of one of these war-bonnets. The head of the female idol with the War-god has the terraced rain-cloud so common on female idols.

all the snakes they could carry darted down to the mesa side and distributed them to the cardinal points. A shower of spittle from the assembled spectators followed them, much to the discomfort of those who did not happen to be on the housetops. This habit of expectorating after those bearing important prayers is also noticeable in the Niman-katcina, or Departure of the Katcinas, and may be considered as a form of prayer for benefits desired. Before the reptiles which had been thrown into this ring of meal had been seized by the priests they crawled together and the girls and women threw what meal remained in their plaques upon the writhing mass. Some of the spectators were likewise observed to throw pinches of meal in that direction. This is a symbolic prayer which will later be discussed. After the reptiles had been seized by the Snake men and carried down the mesa, one or two persons, among others a Navaho woman, scraped up some of this meal from the ground. About sixty reptiles were used, of which more than a half were rattlesnakes.

The reptiles are carried in the mouths of the Snake priests at Mishongnovi in the same manner as at Walpi, hence the descriptions of the functions of carrier, hugger, and gatherer in the Walpi variant will serve very well for the same personages at Mishongnovi. With minor differences in ceremonial paraphernalia and symbolism, the public Antelope and Snake dances in the largest pueblo of the Middle mesa and at Walpi are identical.

One of the Snake priests did not obtain any of the snakes in the rush for them as they lay on the ground. He seized, however, a large snake which a fellow priest held and for a moment there was a mild struggle for the possession of it, with apparently some ill feeling. But at last he gave it up, and after his companions had departed he made several circuits of the plaza alone, each time stamping on the plank before the kisi, and then marched off. In an account of the termination of the Shumopovi Snake dance of 1896, a similar failure of Snake men to obtain reptiles at the final mêlée is mentioned. It is apparently not regarded an honor to depart from the kisi at the close of the dance without a snake, and in both instances some merriment was expressed by the native spectators at the man who had left the plaza empty-handed.

After the reptiles had been deposited in the fields the Snake men returned to the pueblo, took the "emetic," vomited (plate LI), and partook of the great feast with which the Snake dance in the Hopi pueblos always closes.

SNAKE DANCE AT WALPI IN 1897

Several of the more important features of the Walpi Snake dance were witnessed in 1897, and a few new facts were discovered regarding obscure parts of this variant. In the year named, the author sought especially to notice any innovations or variations from the presentations in 1891, 1893, and 1895, which might result from deaths in the ranks of the celebrants and the increase in the number of white spectators.

The kiva exhibitions were found to remain practically unchanged, and notes made in 1891 might serve equally well as a description of the rite in 1897, although the participants had changed. The mortality among the Antelope priests since the dance was first studied in 1891 has been great, among those who died being Hahawe, Nasyuñweve, Masaiumtiwa, and Intiwa—practically all the older members except Wiki. This has led in some instances to the introduction of lads to fill out the complement of numbers, and with them has come some loss of seriousness in the kiva exercises. For an unknown reason Hoñyi took the part of a Snake priest, and old Tcoshoniwû (Tcino), after several years of absence, resumed his rôle of asperger of the kisi. With the death of the older men of this society much ancient lore concerning the Snake-dance legend has been lost, for the boys who have taken their places are too young to understand or indeed to care much for the ceremony, even if its significance could be explained to them. Wiki, the Antelope chief (plate L), is so deaf that it is next to impossible to communicate with him on the subject, so that much of the Walpi Snake lore is lost forever.

WASHING THE REPTILES

The exercises in the Snake kiva during the washing of the snakes were practically identical with those elsewhere described, and therefore need not be repeated: but an exceptional event occurred at the end of the rite: One of the reptiles had crawled up the side of the room above the spectators' part and had hidden in a hole in the roof, so that only a small part of the scaly body could be seen. An attempt was first made to dig the snake out from the inside of the room, but as that was not successful some of the men went outside on the roof, and were obliged to remove some of the stones before the reptile was captured. It was finally brought down the ladder and washed with the others.

Supela was followed out of the kiva in order to note more in detail than hitherto what was done with the liquid in which the snakes had been bathed, and with the altar sand in which they had been dried (plate LII). He went through the western court of Walpi to the end of the mesa, and, standing on the edge of the cliff, poured a little of the water over it in four places. Although his explanation of this act was not very lucid, the rite is undoubtedly connected in some way with world-quarters worship. The bowl in which the snakes had been washed was later deposited, with the jars in which they had been kept, in a crypt on the northern side of the mesa. As these jars must not be profaned by any secular use, they are deposited in a special cave, as is the figurine of Talatumsi used in the New-fire rites.

INFLUENCE OF WHITE SPECTATORS

The number of white spectators of the Walpi Snake dance in 1897 was more than double that during any previous dance, and probably two hundred would not be far from the actual enumeration. An audience of this size, with the addition of various Navaho and the residents of Walpi and neighboring pueblos, is too large for the size of the plaza, and it became a matter of grave concern to those who are familiar with the mode of construction of the walls and roofs of the pueblo whether they would support the great weight which they were called upon to bear (plate LV). Happily these fears proved to be groundless, but if the spectators increase in number in the next presentations as rapidly as in the past, it will hardly be possible for the pueblo to accommodate them.

The influx of white spectators has had its influence on the native performers, for, when gazed upon by so many strangers, some of the Snake men appeared to be more nervous, and did not handle the reptiles in the fearless manner which marked earlier performances. The older members of the fraternity maintained the same earnestness, but the more youthful glanced so often at the spectators that their thoughts seemed to be on other subjects than the solemn duty before them, and they dodged the fallen reptiles in a way not before seen at Walpi. A proposition to perform the dance at Albuquerque, New Mexico, in 1897, was entertained by the young men, but was promptly refused by the chiefs. Germs of a degeneration of the religious character of the Walpi Snake dance have thus began to develop. When the old men pass away it may be that an attempt to induce the Snake priests to perform their dance for gain will be successful; but when that time comes the Snake dance will cease to be a religious ceremony, the secret rites will disappear, and nothing remain but a spectacular show.

UNUSUAL FEATURES

During the public exhibition of the Walpi Snake dance in 1897 several of the priests carried a tiny snake with the head protruding from the mouth like a cigar. Kopeli explained this by saying that he had found a brood of young snakes, but that they were not put in the cottonwood bower on account of their small size and the consequent difficulty in finding them. They were therefore held in the performers' mouths from the time they left their kiva.

The author's attention was called by one or two of the spectators to the fact that one of the Snake priests was bitten during the dance, but when the chief was asked for the name of the man bitten no information

PARTICIPANTS TAKING THE EMETIC AT WALPI

PHOTOGRAPH BY MAUDE AND JAMES

M Wright Gill.

SUPELA AT ENTRANCE TO WALPI SNAKE KIVA

in that respect could be elicited; he declared that no one had been bitten during the exhibition. One of the writer's party says that he saw one of the Snake priests with a small frog in his mouth, which is apropos of a statement by a responsible Indian that in former times other animals than snakes were carried by the priests in their mouths. Subsequent interrogations of the chief failed to make known the man who carried the frog in the way indicated.

NUMBER OF PARTICIPANTS

An enumeration of the participants in the last four performances of the Walpi Snake dance shows that the number is gradually increasing. The Snake society has become a very popular one, possibly on account of the increase in the number of visitors. Several young men of Walpi wish to join, and a man at the Middle Mesa declared that while he did not care to become a member of the Snake society of his own pueblo he would much like to be enrolled among the followers of Kopeli. The gradual increase in the number of participants certainly does not show a decline in the popularity of the Snake dance, or that it is likely soon to be abandoned. The religious element, in which the ethnologist has the greatest interest, will be the first to disappear. In all the Tusayan pueblos, save Walpi, the number of Antelope priests is about the same as that of Snake priests; but at Walpi there are over twice as many Snake as Antelope priests. It is evident that this predominance is due to the popularity of the society (since the clan is no larger in Walpi than in the other pueblos), and may be traced directly to the influx of visitors to witness the spectacular performance; but while the number of Antelope priests at Walpi has diminished, that of the Snake priests has steadily increased.[1]

WOMEN MEMBERS OF THE SNAKE SOCIETY

The women members of the Snake society are so numerous that Kopeli did not pretend to count them or to be able to mention their names. They never take part in the public Snake dance, except by sprinkling meal on the participants, but join the society and offer their children for initiation as a protection against rattlesnake bites and for the additional benefit of the invocations in the kiva performances. There are also women members of the Antelope society, but they are not so numerous as in the Snake society. These women belong to several clans, and the membership of women in both societies is a survival of ancient times when all members (females as well as males) of the Horn and Snake clans were members of the Antelope and Snake societies.

---

[1] A count of the Snake priests in 1891 indicated 41, and there were 4 novices that year. The author omitted to note the number of novices in 1893, 1895, and 1897, but counted 50 Snake priests in 1897.

PHOTOGRAPHS OF THE WALPI SNAKE DANCE

During the last five performances the Snake dances in the Hopi pueblos have been photographed again and again, with varying success. Although the conditions of light at the time of the dance are poor, there has been a steady improvement at each successive presentation, and fine views can now be purchased from various photographers. The author has made a collection of these views, most of which were presented by the photographers, and has selected some of the more instructive for illustration in this article.

THE WALPI ANTELOPE ALTAR

The accompanying illustration (plate LIII) shows the Antelope altar at Walpi on the ninth day of the Snake dance. It was based on an excellent photograph made by Mr George Wharton James, who has kindly allowed me to make use of his photographic work. The plate differs from the photograph in several respects, for on the day (Totokya) on which the latter was taken several objects, as the two tiponis, were absent, and the sand mosaic was imperfectly represented. These two features are restored in the illustration.

TIPONIS

Of all objects on a Hopi altar perhaps the most important and constant is the badge of office or palladium, known as the tiponi, of the religious society which celebrates the rites about it. The Antelope altar has for the first seven days two tiponis, the Snake and Antelope. When the Snake altar is constructed the Snake tiponi is taken from the Antelope kiva to the Snake kiva, where it forms the essential object of the new altar. The two tiponis are shown in plate LIII at the middle of the side of the altar, on the border of the sand picture next to the kiva wall. The two tiponis are separated by a stone fetish of the mountain lion. These two objects of the societies, called "mothers," are the most sacred objects which the altars contain, and their presence shows that the altars are the legitimate ones. Each is deposited on a small mound of sand upon which six radiating lines of sacred meal are drawn by the chief.

STONE IMAGES OF ANIMALS

There were several stone images of animals on the Antelope altar at Walpi, which were distributed as follows on the western border of the sand mosaic near the tiponis: the largest, representing a mountain lion, stood between the two palladia of the society. It was upon this fetish that Wiki rested his conical pipe when he made the great rain-cloud smoke after the eighth song in the sixteen-songs ceremony, as elsewhere[1] fully described.

---

[1] Journal of American Ethnology and Archæology, vol. IV.

PHOTOGRAPH BY MAUDE AND JAMES

KAKAPTI AT ENTRANCE TO WALPI ANTELOPE KIVA

ANTELOPE ALTAR AT WALPI

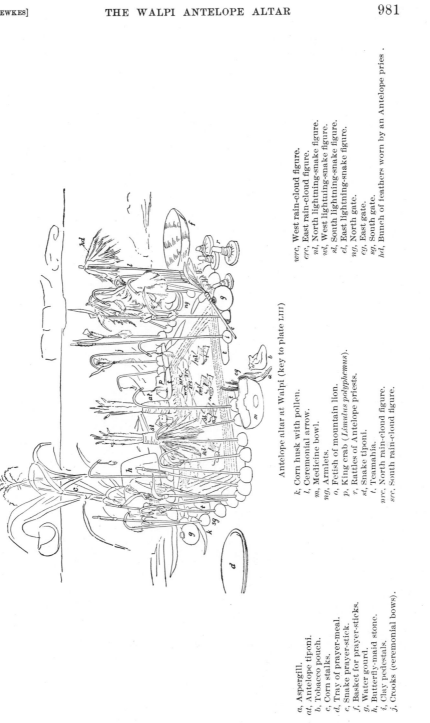

Antelope altar at Walpi (key to plate LIII)

a, Aspergill.
al, Antelope tiponi.
b, Tobacco pouch.
c, Corn stalks.
d, Tray of prayer-meal.
e, Snake prayer-stick.
f, Basket for prayer-sticks.
g, Water gourd.
h, Butterfly-maid stone.
i, Clay pedestals.
j, Crooks (ceremonial bows).

k, Corn husk with pollen.
l, Ceremonial arrow.
m, Medicine bowl.
ng, Armlets.
o, Fetish of mountain lion.
p, King crab (Limulus polyphemus).
r, Rattles of Antelope priests.
sl, Snake tiponi.
t, Tcamahia.
nrc, North rain-cloud figure.
src, South rain-cloud figure.

wrc, West rain-cloud figure.
erc, East rain-cloud figure.
nl, North lightning-snake figure.
wl, West lightning-snake figure.
sl, South lightning-snake figure.
el, East lightning-snake figure.
ng, North gate.
eg, East gate.
sg, South gate.
hd, Bunch of feathers worn by an Antelope pries .

There were also three smaller stone animals, which belonged to Wiki, in a row by the side of the Antelope tiponi; and an equal number, the property of the Snake chief, placed in a similar way by the side of his tiponi. When the Snake chief makes his altar in the Snake kiva he takes his three animal fetishes and his tiponi from the Antelope altar and deposits them on his own altar.

TCAMAHIA

The row of flat stone implements called tcamahia was arranged around the border of the sand picture, there being on each of three sides a midway opening called a gate. There were eighteen of these objects. They were of smooth light-brown stone, similar to those often excavated from ancient Arizona ruins. Those on the northern and southern sides were regarded as male, the eastern and western ones as female tcamahia. They were looked upon as ancient weapons, representing the Warrior or Puma clan of the Snake phratry.

The displaced tcamahia on the right side of the sand picture, near a gap or gateway in the row of pedestals on that side, was the stone implement which Kakapti used in rapping on the floor as an accompaniment to one of the sixteen songs, as has been elsewhere described.[1]

It should be noted that the name of these ancient stone objects is identical with the opening words of the invocation which the asperger utters before the kisi in the public Snake dance. These words are Keresan, and are used in ceremonies of the Sia,[2] but their signification was not divulged by the Hopi priests. It is probable that we have here, as often happens in ancient customs, a designation of stone implements by the name applied to them by the people who originally used them.

STICKS ABOUT THE SAND MOSAIC

The sticks which are placed about the sand picture are of two kinds, some having a crook at the end, the others being straight throughout. The arrangement of these sticks may be seen in the accompanying plate LIII, where they are shown placed in clay pedestals on the outer margin of the sand mosaic.

The sticks provided with a crook have attached to them a string with a breast feather of an eagle, stained red. The straight sticks, called arrows, have more complicated appendages, for to their upper ends are attached a packet of meal, a feather, and a dried corn leaf. The bundles of feathers represented in the plate as fastened to the ends of these sticks are those which the priests wear on their heads during the public dances. These bundles are not found on the sticks

---

[1] Snake ceremonials at Walpi, Journal American Ethnology and Archæology, vol. IV, p. 34.
[2] Mrs. M. C. Stevenson, The Sia, Eleventh Annual Report of the Bureau of Ethnology. Mrs. Stevenson mentions similar words used in invocations to the warriors of the cardinal points.

during the first days of the ceremony; they are not essential to the efficacy of the altar, but are hung as indicated because of the sacred influence which is supposed to be imparted to them through this association.   For the same reason there are placed on the altar the several rattles seen on the right-hand corner, as well as the netted water gourds which appear here only on the last two days of the Snake ceremony, in the public dances of which they are used.   Two objects to the right of the tiponi, on the rear margin of the sand mosaic, have been added to the altar fetishes since the celebration of 1891.   They occupied the position named during the 1893, 1895, and 1897 celebrations.   One of these is the cephalothorax of a king crab (*Limulus polyphemus*), the other a fragment of water-worn wood.   Both of these were gifts from the author to Wiki, the Antelope chief, in 1893.

MEDICINE BOWL AND ASPERGILL

The medicine bowl and aspergill are shown in the illustration near the front margin of the altar, to the right of the eastern "gateway" or passage through the row of crooks on that side.   The aspergill consists of two feathers tied by a leather thong.   By its side is a bag of tobacco.   The two whizzers are flat slats of wood with rain-cloud terraces cut in the end.

OTHER OBJECTS ON THE ALTAR

On the right side of the altar, near a netted gourd, there were two corn husks, one of which contained corn meal, the other pollen for the use of the priests who sat on this side of the altar.   On the same side, back of the altar, is seen the slab called the Hokona-mana or Butterfly-virgin slab, upon which are depicted butterflies, rain clouds, falling rain, and tadpoles, as has been described in a previous memoir.[1]   Near the "gateway" or passage between the crooks, on the right side of the altar, is a rattle upon which two wristlets made of bark are laid. The pointed stick leaning upon a water gourd to the left of the opening through the row of crooks, in front of the alter, is a Snake paho, or prayer-stick, to one end of which are attached a dried corn leaf, a twig of sagebrush, feathers, and a corn-husk packet of sacred meal. The four markings which encircle the corn husk at its attachment to the stick are well shown in the illustration.   The flat Havasupai basket to the right of the altar is the one in which the prayer-sticks are placed during the singing of the sixteen songs.   The basket was empty when the photograph of the altar was made, for the prayer sticks had just been delivered to Kakapti to carry to the four world-quarter shrines.

---

[1] Journal of American Ethnology and Archæology, vol. iv.

ANTELOPE PRIESTS IN THE PUBLIC DANCE

Twelve Antelope priests lined up near the kisi in the Walpi Snake dance of 1897 (plate LV). Eight of these stood on the same side of the cottonwood bower at the Snake rock, while four were on the opposite side. All the former were adults, and three of the latter were boys. It will at once be noticed that there is a difference in the adornment and bodily markings of the adult Antelope priests. This variation is believed to be of significance, probably being connected with the clans to which the participants belong.

Following are the names of the Antelope priests who took part in the public dance:

1. Tcoshoniwû (Tcino). This man acted as the asperger, calling out the foreign word "tcamahia" at the kisi. He wore on his head a fillet of green cottonwood leaves and a white ceremonial kilt bound about his waist with a knotted cord. His face was not painted, nor was his chin blackened; and the white marginal line from the upper lip to the ears, so typical of the Antelope priests, did not appear. He carried a medicine bowl and an aspergill, but no rattle. His body was not decorated with zigzag lines, which are so conspicuous on the chest, back, arms, and legs of the Antelope chief. Tcoshoniwû took no part in the secret rites of either the Antelope or the Snake priests, and he appeared only in the public exhibitions. He belongs to the Patki (Water-house) clan.

2. Wiki stood next in line, and as he is the Antelope chief his dress and bodily decoration were typical of the priests of that society. He wore on his head a small white feather, and his chin was painted black with a bordering white line from the ears to the upper lip. He wore a white ceremonial kilt with a knotted sash, and also moccasins and armlets. On both breasts down to the abdomen, and on his back, arms, thighs, and legs were zigzag lines in white. He carried a rattle in his right hand, a basket tray of sacred meal in his left, and on his left arm rested the Antelope palladium, or Tcüb-tiponi. Wiki belongs to the Snake clan and is an uncle of Kopeli, the Snake chief.

3. Katci: The bodily decoration of this priest was like that of the Antelope chief, except that he wore a bunch of variegated feathers in his hair. He carried a stick in the left and a rattle in the right hand, and wore armlets in which cottonwood boughs were inserted. Katci is chief of the Kokop, or Firewood, clan.

4, 5. Pontima and Kwaa: The faces of these two men were painted differently from those of Wiki or Katci; their chins were not blackened, nor was a white line painted from the upper lip to the ears. Their chests were decorated with two parallel white bands, instead of zigzag lines characteristic of Antelope priests. Their forearms and legs were painted white, but not in zigzag designs. They wore embroidered anklets, but were without moccasins. Bunches of variegated feathers were attached to their scalps. Each carried a paho in the left hand and a rattle in the right hand, and wore a white buck-skin across the shoulders. Four hanks of yarn were tied about their left knees. Pontima belongs to the Ala (Horn); Kwaa to the Patki (Water-house).

6. Kakapti: The dress and bodily decoration of Kakapti resembled those of Katci, but he had a bowstring guard on his left wrist. Kakapti belongs to the Tüwa, or Sand, clan.

7, 8. ———: These men, as well as the three boys who stood on the left of the kisi, were dressed and painted like Kakapti. They carried similar objects in their hands.

9. Wikyatiwa: This man was clothed and painted differently from any other Antelope priest. He wore a white ceremonial kilt and sash; over his shoulder hung a buckskin and a quiver with bow and arrows. From the back of his head there was suspended a bundle of feathers tied to a bone spearpoint by a leather thong. He bore in his left hand two whizzers and at times twirled one of these with his right arm. He also carried in his left hand the so-called awata-natci, a bow with appended horsehair and feathers, which hung on the ladder during the secret rites in the Antelope kiva (plate XLIX). Upon each cheek there was a daub of white pigment, and a mark on each forearm, thigh, and leg. Wikyatiwa personated a kalektaka, or warrior, or Püükoñ, the cultus hero of the Kalektaka society or Priesthood of the Bow.

The objective symbolism of Tcoshoniwû, or Tcino, the asperger, led me to suppose that he personated the ancestral Tcamahia, the ancient people who parted from the Snake clans at Wukoki and whose descendants are said to live at Acoma.

Pontima and Kwaa, who were adorned and clothed unlike Wiki, the typical Antelope priest, show later symbolism due to contact with other than Snake clans, and suggest katcina influences. Pontima took the place of Hahawe (Ala clan), who was similarly painted in 1891 but who died in 1893.

An examination of the platoon of Antelope priests, as they lined up at Oraibi and Mishongnovi, failed to reveal any persons dressed simi-larly to the priests numbered 4 and 5 of the Walpi line. It appears, therefore, that we must regard this as a significant difference in the public exercises in the different Tusayan pueblos. It will also be borne in mind that in the Oraibi Snake dance the asperger, like all the other Antelopes, has white zigzag lines on his chest, and that none of the Antelope priests in the dance at Oraibi were observed to have armlets with inserted cottonwood boughs. There is, however, a close resemblance in the dress and bodily decoration of all the Antelope priests in all the pueblos except Walpi, a fact which tells in favor of the idea that the more primitive form of the ceremony is found at Oraibi and in the Middle mesa villages.

THE MOST PRIMITIVE SNAKE DANCE

We have now sufficient data regarding the five variants of the Hopi Snake dance to enable us to consider the question which one of them is most primitive or more nearly like the ancestral performance. There is no doubt which is the largest and most complex, for the Walpi performance easily holds that position; and there is no other pueblo where the influence of white men is so pronounced, especially in the paraphernalia of the participants in the public dance. To these innovations the prosperity of the East mesa people, due to their intercourse with civilization, has contributed largely. The three pueblos on the East mesa are, or have been, more frequently visited, and, as a rule, their inhabitants are more liberally disposed to improvements of all kinds than are those of Oraibi and the Middle mesa. As a result we should expect the Walpi ritual to be more greatly modified than that of any other Hopi village, and we may therefore suppose that the Snake dances of Oraibi and the Middle Mesa are nearer to the ancestral form.

It is not alone that the white man's civilization has acted more profoundly on Walpi than on more isolated Oraibi; the former pueblo is nearer Zuñi and the other New Mexican villages, and was naturally more greatly affected by outside contact before the advent of white men. The Hopi population gained many increments from the Rio Grande before the white man's influence began.

The coming of the Tanoan class of Hano exerted a liberalizing tendency on the adjacent pueblos, for their ancestors came to Tusayan with a more intimate knowledge of white people than the Hopi could have gained at that time. These Tewa received the Americans more hospitably than did the true Hopi. Men of Hano moved down from the mesa to the foothills and the plain when urged by governmental officials, braving the threats and superstitious forebodings of the more conservative people of Walpi. They have for the last twenty years exerted a liberalizing influence on Hopi relations with the United States, and that ever-growing influence has greatly reduced the conservatism of Walpi and Sichumovi.[1] Such an influence has not existed to the same extent at Oraibi and among the Middle Mesa villages. One needs but visit the three clusters of Hopi pueblos and note their present condition to see that the inhabitants of those on the East mesa are far ahead of the others in the adoption of new secular customs, and this influence can be seen in their ritual, leading to the belief that the oldest variants of ceremonies persist at Oraibi and the Middle mesa.

---

[1] In 1890 there were only two houses in the foothills under the East mesa and these were inhabited by Tewa families. There was not a single house at the base of the Middle mesa and Oraibi. At the present writing the foothills and plains are dotted with new houses of the white man's type.

PHOTOGRAPH BY MAUDE AND JAMES

ANTELOPE PRIESTS AT WALPI

CRYPT IN WHICH SNAKE JARS ARE KEPT AT MISHONGNOVI

FLUTE CEREMONY AT MISHONGNOVI IN 1896

The Leñya or Flute ceremony is one of the most complicated in the Hopi ritual, and one of the most important in the calendar. It occurs in five pueblos, not being celebrated at Sichumovi or at Hano. The ceremony was first described by the author in an article[1] in which the public rites or "dance" at Walpi were briefly noted and their relation to the Snake dance was first recognized. When this paper was published the author was unaware that the Flute ceremony was of nine days' duration, for in 1890, when the description was written, the existence of nine days ceremonies among the Hopi was unknown. A more extended study of the Hopi ritual in the following year (1891) revealed the fact that a Flute ceremony, similar to that at Walpi, occurred likewise in the four other Hopi pueblos which celebrate the complete ritual, and in 1892 the author described the last two days of the Flute rite at Shipaulovi. In the course of these studies it was recognized that this ceremony lasted nine days, that it was performed by two divisions of Flute priests, and that each division had an elaborate altar about which secret rites were performed.

The author was the first to recognize that several of the great Hopi ceremonies, as the Lalakoñti, Mamzrauti, Flute, and others, extend through nine days, and that the Snake ceremony has the same duration. Whether or not the other pueblo rituals have similar time limits to individual ceremonies is not clear from the fragmentary descriptions which have been published.

The increased knowledge of the intricate character of the Flute ceremony led to a detailed study of the Walpi variant, and with the aid of the late A. M. Stephen the author was enabled to publish[2] a number of new facts on the Flute ceremony at Walpi in 1892. The only account of the Oraibi variant of the Flute ceremony that has been given is a description of the altars, which appeared in 1895,[3] being a record of observations made on a limited visit to that pueblo in the summer of the year named. In the following year this account was supplemented by a memoir on the Flute altars of Mishongnovi.

It will thus be seen that there exist published accounts of the Flute altars of all the Hopi pueblos except Shumopovi, and fragmentary descriptions of the secret and public exercises in two pueblos, Walpi and Shipaulovi. The following description of the Flute exercises at Mishognovi supplement those already given and add to our knowledge of the rites of the Flute society in the largest village of the Middle mesa. It will be noticed, by a comparison of these rites, that at Mishongnovi they are more complicated than similar ceremonies

---

[1] Journal of American Folk-Lore, vol. IV, number 13.
[2] Op. cit., vol. VII, number 26.
[3] Op. cit., number 31.

at Walpi and Shipaulovi, but less so than those at Oraibi. No complete account of the observance of this ceremony at Oraibi and Shumopovi has been published, although it has been witnessed in the former pueblo by many Americans.

Flute Rooms

It is a significant fact that none of the secret rites of the Flute priests in any of the pueblos are, so far as is known, performed in kivas, but occur in ancestral rooms of the Flute clan. Although this is unusual in Hopi secret rites, it is not exceptional, for there are at least two other very important secret rites on the East mesa which are not performed in kivas. Since it is true, therefore, that at present a kiva is not the essential or necessarily prescribed place in which secret rites are performed, and as the ceremonies observed in living rooms are also said to be ancient, this fact may explain the absence of kivas in many Arizona ruins. Whatever the explanation, it shows that the absence of a kiva, or room set apart for secret rites, does not prove the nonexistence of an elaborate ritual.

Possibly these facts may shed light on the relative antiquity of circular and rectangular sacred rooms, or kivas, the former of which do not exist in Tusayan. Mindeleff says that "there is no doubt that the circular form is the most primitive, and was formerly used by some tribes which now have only the rectangular form." This may be true of some parts of the Pueblo area, especially in New Mexico, from San Juan river southward, where circular kivas are a marked architectural feature; but in Arizona, from Utah to the Mexican boundary, no circular kiva has been found. There is nothing to lead us to suppose that circular kivas in the former region antedated those of rectangular shape, or that New Mexican clans once had them. It seems more likely that the secret rites were once performed in ordinary rectangular rooms, or dwelling chambers, of the same shape as those now called kivas, which ultimately were given up wholly to ceremonial purposes. The Flute rooms are believed to be survivals of a time before this differentiation, which was brought about by the enlargement of the religious society by the initiation of men of other clans, through which means the fraternity outgrew the ancestral dwelling.

Ceremonial Days of the Rite

There are nine active days of the Flute ceremony, which are designated by the names given in the following list. The author has studied the proceedings of the last day, called Tihune, the day of personation.

August 7, Yuñya.	August 12, Soskahimu.
August 8, Custala.	August 13, Komoktotokya.
August 9, Luctala.	August 14, Totokya.
August 10, Paictala.	August 15, Tihune.
August 11, Natuctala.	

The Mishongnovi Flute Altars

There were two Flute altars at Mishongnovi, one called the Cakwaleñya (Blue Flute), the other Macileñya (Drab Flute). The chief of
the Cakwaleñya had a tiponi on his altar, but although the chief of
the Drab Flute had one of these sacred palladia in the room, it was
not in its customary position on the altar. The author noticing this
fact, asked to see his tiponi. The chief showed it, unwinding its
wrappings, but failed to explain satisfactorily why he did not set it in
its proper place. The only explanation of this failure is a theoretical
one, that the tiponi was not a true Drab Flute palladium. Walpi
has, as is known, no Drab Flute tiponi, and as there is close resemblance between ceremonies at Walpi and Mishongnovi, it would not
be strange if the same were true of the latter pueblo. Both Oraibi
and Shipaulovi have this badge, which will probably likewise be found
in Shumopovi. It would seem that subordinate societies may celebrate
their part of a rite without a chieftain's badge, but the celebration is
on that account lacking in ardor. This is the case with the Snake dance
in Tusayan, which is nowhere celebrated with so much fervor as at
Walpi; for in all the five villages which hold this festival there is but
one Snake tiponi, that of the Snake chief at Walpi.

The reredos of the Macileñya altar (figure 43) consisted of two uprights supporting a flat wooden arch. The uprights were incised with
three rows of concave depressions arranged vertically. The tranverse
portion, or arch, bore four figures of rain clouds outlined by black
borders, from which depended a row of parallel black lines representing falling rain. The lower third of the arch had two rows of concavities, similar to those on the uprights. The reredos stood in front
of a bank of maize stacked at the end of the room, a feature common to
all Flute altars, but not shown in the accompanying illustration. The
parts of the altar were tied together with yucca shreds, and were held
in place with wooden pegs. On the floor at the right-hand side of the
altar, leaning against the wall, there were two rectangular tiles, each
of which was decorated with rain-cloud symbols and dragonflies.

Two figurines were set on small heaps of sand in front of the reredos—one on the right, called the Flute youth; the other on the left,
the Flute maid. These figurines were armless effigies, with prominent lateral appendages to the head in the place of ears. Each of these
appendages was tipped with radiating rods connected by red yarn,
and resembled a symbolic squash blossom. The cheeks bore triangular
markings. Six feathers, three on each side, projected at right angles
from the sides of the body, and a narrow painted band, consisting of
alternate blocks of black and white, was made along the medial line,
extending from a symbolic figure of a rain cloud upon which half an
ear of maize was painted. These two figurines are similar in position
and shape to the effigies on other Flute altars, as elsewhere described,

and have the same names.   Just in front of the figurines, one on each
side, were placed short, thick, upright sticks, rounded at the top and
pierced with holes, from which, like pins from a cushion, projected
small rods tipped with flaring ends painted in several colors, representing flowers.   These sticks correspond to the mounds of sand, covered with meal, of other Flute altars, and are called talastcomos.   The
mounds admit of the following explanation: In many stories of the origin of societies of priests which took place in the underworld, the first
members are represented as erecting their altars before the "flower
mound" of Müiyiñwû.   This was the case of the Flute youth and

Fig. 43—Altar of the Macileñya at Mishongnovi.

Flute maid, progenitors of the Flute Society.   These mounds, now
erected on earth before the figurine of Müiyiñwü in the Flute chambers, symbolize the ancestral mounds of the underworld, the wooden
objects inserted in them representing flowers.

The interval between the uprights of the reredos was occupied by a
number of zigzag sticks or rods (symbolic of lightning), cornstalks,
and other objects.

These rods and sticks, as well as the uprights themselves, were held
vertically by a ridge of sand on the floor.   From the middle of this
ridge, half way from each end and at right angles to the altar, there

was spread on the floor a zone of sand upon which meal had been
sprinkled.   This zone terminated at the end opposite the reredos with
a short bank of sand at right angles to it, in which an upright row of
eagle-wing feathers was set.   Upon the zone of sand there was placed
a row of rudely carved bird effigies, and at the extremity of this row,
just before the eagle-wing feathers, stood a slab upon which was
depicted half an ear of maize and two rain-cloud symbols, one of the
latter being on each side.   Between the first bird effigy and the slab
was a medicine bowl, from which the nearest bird appeared to be

FIG. 44—Altar of the Cakwaleñya at Mishongnovi.

drinking.   The bird effigies were eight in number, all facing from
the altar.   There were likewise on the floor other ceremonial paraphernalia common to all altars, among which may be mentioned
the six-directions maize (corn of six colors used in a six-directions
altar), rattles, a medicine bowl, a basket-tray of sacred meal, a honey
pot, and similar objects.   Their position on the floor by the altar is
not significant.

The altar of the Cakwaleñya society (figure 44) was even more
complicated.   Its reredos consisted of uprights and transverse slats of

wood, the former decorated with ten rain-cloud pictures, five on each side, one above the other. These symbols had square outlines, each angle decorated with a figure of a feather, and depending from each rain-cloud figure, parallel lines, representing falling rain, were painted. The transverse slat bore a row of nine rain-cloud figures of semicircular form. Four zigzag sticks, representing lightning, hung from the transverse slat between the vertical or lateral parts of the reredos. Two supplementary uprights were fastened to the main reredos, one on each side. These were decorated at their bases with symbolic pictures representing maize, surmounted by rain-cloud figures. The ridge of sand between the uprights of the altar supported many smaller rods and slats, the one in the middle being decorated with a picture of an ear of corn.

From the middle point of this ridge of sand a wide trail of sand, covered with meal, was drawn across the floor at right angles to the altar. This zone terminated abruptly, and upon it was placed a row of four bird effigies, all facing from the altar. Between the second and third bird was a small bowl. A tiponi stood at the left of the sand zone, looking toward the altar, and at the left of this were two water gourds alternating with ears of corn.

Three figurines stood before the altar, one on the left, and two on the right side. The figurine on the left represented the Flute youth, who held in both hands a miniature flute upon which he appeared to be playing. On his head was a corn-husk packet, and around his neck a necklace of artificial flowers. Of the two figurines on the other side, one represented the flute maid, the other Müiyiñwû. The latter had an ear of maize depicted on each of the four sides of the body. Upon her head were three rain-cloud symbols, and her cheeks were decorated with triangular markings. On the floor in front of the two smaller figurines were hillocks of sand, into which were inserted small rods with trumpet-like extremities variously colored.

Although the author did not witness the secret ceremonials of either of the Flute societies at Mishongnovi, for want of time, he saw from the nature of the prayer-sticks (pahos) that they probably resembled the rites at Shipaulovi. In addition to the prescribed Flute pahos he observed the manufacture of the two wooden slabs, decorated with corn figures, which were carried by the maidens in the public dance, and the balls of clay with small sticks, called the tadpoles, which are made in both the Flute and the Snake ceremonies at Walpi. There is close resemblance between the small natcis, or Flute pahos, tied to the ladder of each of the Flute houses, and the awata-natcis, or standards, with skins and red-stained horsehair, that are placed on the roofs of the chambers in which the altars are erected.

COMPARISON WITH THE WALPI FLUTE ALTAR

As has been already pointed out, there is but one Flute altar at Walpi, that of the Cakwaleñya, the Macileñya society having become extinct. The uprights of the reredos in the flute altars of both pueblos bear similar symbolic pictures of rain clouds, five in number, one above the other. The transverse slat, or the arch, of the Walpi Flute altar differs from that of the Mishongnovi in having a picture of Tawa (sun), with two semicircular rain-cloud figures on each side, in the interval between which is pictured a zigzag figure representing lightning. Both altars have images of the Flute youth, Flute maid, and Müiyiñwû, and so far as is known they are the only Tusayan Flute altars which have an effigy of the personage last mentioned. The Walpi figurine of the Flute youth has no flute in his hand, and the slabs with figures of persons playing the flute, elsewhere described, which characterize the Walpi altar, are not found at Mishongnovi.

COMPARISON WITH THE ORAIBI FLUTE ALTARS [1]

The uprights of the reredos of the Drab Flute altar at Oraibi have the same rows of concavities on their front surfaces as have those at Mishongnovi, and are without the rain-cloud symbols seen on the transverse slat; but instead of having a row of concave depressions on its lower half, the transverse part of the Oraibi reredos is in the form of a rain-cloud, ornamented with differently colored cloud symbols, one above another, with accompanying representations of lightning and figures of birds. No other Flute altar known to the author has a more elaborate reredos than that of the Macileñya at Oraibi. In common with the Drab Flute altar at Mishongnovi it has two effigies of the cultus heroes of the society, the Flute youth and the Flute maid; but the most remarkable statuette of the Oraibi altar was that of Cotokinuñwû, which stood with outstretched arms in a conspicuous position. No other known Flute altar has a figurine of this personage, although it is possibly represented by the zigzag lightning-sticks hanging between the uprights of the reredos.

The so-called flower mounds, or hillocks of sand beset with artificial flowers, before the figures of the cultus heroes of the Oraibi altar differ in form from those at Mishongnovi, although they evidently have the same significance. At Oraibi these flowers are fastened to a common stalk, while at Mishongnovi their stems are inserted in a log of wood, and at Shipaulovi in a mound of sand.

Perhaps the most marked difference between the Drab Flute altar of Oraibi and that of Mishongnovi is the presence on the floor of the former of a mosaic made of kernels of maize of different colors representing a rain-cloud; in this feature it differs from all other

---

[1] The Mishongnovi Drab Flute altar has certain likenesses to the Oraibi Flute altar elsewhere described. Journal of American Folk-Lore, vol. VIII, number 31.

19 ETH, PT 2——28

altars known to the author.   This mosaic occupies the position of the zone of sand, and as a consequence the row of birds placed on this zone are, in Oraibi, found in two clusters, one on each side of the maize mosaic.   There are several objects on the Oraibi Flute altar which are absent from that at Mishongnovi, among which may be noticed a bowl back of the tiponi, wooden objects, artificial flowers like those inserted into the mounds of sand, and panpipe-like objects. The two upright wooden cylindricals representing maize, the rain-cloud symbols between the uprights of the altar, and the statuette of Cotokinuñwû appear to be characteristic of the Oraibi altar.

Markedly different as are the Drab Flute altars of Oraibi and Mishongnovi, those of the Blue Flute are even more divergent.   In fact, they have little in common, and can not readily be compared. The Oraibi altar has no reredos, but paintings on the wall of the chamber serve the same purpose.   The Oraibi altar is composed of a medicine-bowl, placed on the floor and surrounded by six differently-colored ears of maize laid in radiating positions (a six-directions altar), the whole inclosed by a rectangle composed of four banks of sand into which rows of eagle wing-feathers had been inserted.

The reason the Oraibi Cakwaleñya altar is so poor in fetishes would have been found to be paralleled in the Walpi Macileñya altar, now extinct, were we acquainted with its character.   We shall never know what the nature of this altar was, notwithstanding the fact that it fell into disuse within the memory of a chief who died only a few years ago; but the author believes that one reason for its disappearance was that the Macileñya division of the Flute fraternity had no chieftain's badge, or tiponi.[1]

No object corresponding with the bundle of aspergills tied to a rod and set upright in a pedestal, described in my account of the Oraibi Flute altar, was seen in either of the two Flute chambers at Mishongnovi, nor do I recall its homologue in Walpi or Shipaulovi.   As the standard, or awata-natci,[2] stood in the Flute chamber, and not on the roof, when I saw the altar, it is possible that the aspergills belong with this object rather than to the altar itself.

COMPARISON WITH THE SHIPAULOVI FLUTE ALTARS

Both Flute altars at Shipaulovi are simpler than those at Mishongnovi, a feature due in part to the fact that Shipaulovi is a smaller pueblo and is of more modern origin.

The reredos of the Blue Flute altar[3] is composed of a few upright

---

[1] This sacred palladium ("mother") is, as has been repeatedly pointed out, the essential object of the altar, the great fetish of the society.   A religious society destitute of it is weak, and rapidly deteriorates.   Hence the want of virility of the Snake society at Oraibi and the pueblos of the Middle mesa.   Their chiefs have no tiponi and the cult is not vigorous.

[2] The staff is set on the roof to indicate that the altar is erected, and the secret rites in progress in the chamber below.   The term awata-natci, "bow upright," is descriptive of the standard of the Snake and Antelope ceremonials, when a bow and arrows are tied to the kiva ladders (plate XLVII).

[3] See The Oraibi Flute Altar, Journal American Ethnology and Archæology, vol. II.

CAKWALEÑYA SOCIETY OF MISHONGNOVI

MACiLEÑYA SOCIETY OF MISHONGNOVI

slats of wood without a transverse portion. Figurines of the Flute youth and the Flute maid are present, but there is no statuette of Müiyiñwû as at Mishongnovi and Walpi. There are two tiponis and two talastcomos. The sand zone and row of birds are present, and a very characteristic row of rods stands vertically in front of the reredos, where the sticks of zigzag and other forms are found in known Flute altars. In the absence of an upper crosspiece to the reredos the four sticks representing lightning hang from the roof of the room.

The great modifications in the Shipaulovi[1] altar lead the writer to suspect that the altar is more nearly like that of Shumopovi than any other, but until something is known of the altars of the latter pueblo this suggestion may be regarded as tentative.

The altar Macileñya (Drab Flute) at Shipaulovi differs in many respects from that at Mishongnovi, but is in a way comparable with that at Oraibi. The reredos consists of several sticks, some cut into zigzag forms, symbolic of lightning, but there is no transverse slat, as at Mishongnovi and Oraibi. A flat stick upon which is painted a zigzag figure of a lightning snake, elsewhere figured,[2] is interesting in comparison with figures on the Antelope altar at Shumopovi. The four lightning symbols drawn in sand in the mosaic of this altar have horns on their heads, and depending from the angles of the zigzags of the body are triangular appendages, representing turkey feathers, similar to those which are depicted on the Flute slab to which reference is made above. Although the Antelope altar in the Shipaulovi Snake ceremony has no such appendages to the lightning symbols, it is interesting to find these characteristic appendages in symbolic figures used in related ceremonies, where their presence is one more evidence of close relationship between the two pueblos and of the late derivation of the ceremonials of Shipaulovi from Shumopovi.

The position of the image of Cotokinuñwû in the Oraibi Flute altar was occupied, in the Shipaulovi Macileñya altar, by a statuette of Taiowa. Studies of this figurine were not close enough to allow the author to decide whether Taiowa, as represented on the Shipaulovi altar, is the same as Cotokinuñwû, but it is highly probable that the two bear intimate relationship. This figurine is absent from the Oraibi altar, but the pathway or zone of sand, with the birds, the row of feathers, and the decorated slab before it on the Shipaulovi altar are comparable with like parts of a similar altar at Mishongnovi.

There remain undescribed the Flute altars of Shumopovi, the ritual

---

[1] Shipaulovi, "High Peach Place," was founded after the advent of the Spaniards, probably later than 1700. Unlike Mishongnovi and Shumopovi, there is no ruin at the foot of the mesa which is claimed as the former home of the ancestors of this pueblo. Tcukubi, the nearest ruin, appears to have been deserted before the sixteenth century, and the adjacent Payüpki was a Tewa pueblo whose inhabitants left it in a body in the middle of the eighteenth century, and are said to have settled at Sandia, on the Rio Grande.

[2] Journal American Ethnology and Archæology, vol. II, p. 120.

of which pueblo is little known.   These altars are erected in August of every odd year, and figures or descriptions of them would complete our knowledge of Hopi Flute altars.

Public Flute Ceremony

The public dance of the Flute priests at Mishongnovi in 1896 occurred on August 15th, at about 5 p. m., and closely resembled that of Shipaulovi and Walpi.   The preliminary exercises of that day at Toreva spring, which took place just before the march to the pueblo, were not witnessed, but the procession was followed from the time it reached the first terrace of the mesa below the pueblo until it entered the plaza.   As a detailed account of the ceremonies at Toreva spring has been given in a description of the Shipaulovi Flute dance, it will not be necessary to repeat it here.

After the preliminary exercises at the spring a procession was formed which marched to the mesa top along the trail into the pueblo. This procession was aligned in two platoons about thirty feet apart, one called the Cakwaleñya, the other the Macileñya.   The personnel of these platoons was as follows:

PERSONNEL OF CAKWALEÑYA SOCIETY.

The Cakwaleñya society formed the first platoon and was composed of the following personages:
1. The chief.
2. A Flute boy.
3. Two Flute girls.
4. A man wearing a moisture tablet on his back.
5. Four men with white blankets.

The members of this division were arranged as follows: In advance of the procession walked the chief, and directly behind him was the Flute boy with a Flute girl on each side.   The remaining members of the division formed the body of the platoon, flanked by the man with the moisture tablet on his back and a small boy with the Flute standard at his left (plate LVII).

PERSONNEL OF MACILEÑYA SOCIETY.

The Macileñya priests formed the second platoon, which consisted of the following persons:
1. The chief.
2. Flute boy.
3. Two Flute girls.
4. A man with the sun emblem on his back.
5. Men with cornstalks.
6. Five men with white blankets.
7. A naked boy with Flute standard.
8. A warrior.

The arrangement of this division was similar to that of the Cak-waleñya, but it will be noticed that the number of participants was larger. The five men with white blankets walked side by side, while the others, bearing cornstalks, and the man with the sun emblem, formed the left wing of the platoon. A naked boy with the Flute standard accompanied the Macileñya group (plates LVIII, LIX).

THE FLUTE CHIEFS

Each of the Flute chiefs carried his tiponi resting on his left arm, and had a basket-tray of meal in his left hand. He wore a white cere-monial garment, or kilt, with a knotted sash. The chief of the Cakwaleñya is not shown in the accompanying illustration (plate LVII), but the man next to the priest with the sun emblem is the Macileñya chief.

THE FLUTE GIRLS

There were four Flute girls, one on each side of the two Flute boys. They were all clothed alike and bore similar objects in their hands. Each wore a downy feather on the crown of her head, and her hair was tied with a string at the back of the neck. In her ears were square mosaic turquoise pendants, and several necklaces were also worn. The chin was painted black; a white line was drawn across the cheeks from ear to ear along the upper lip. Each girl wore two white blankets, one as a skirt fastened by a girdle having long white pend-ants knotted at the point of attachment. In her left hand she carried objects similar to those borne by the boy, and in the right a small annulet with a loop made of yucca fiber, by which it was slipped over the end of a stick (plate LXI). The dress and facial decoration of the Flute girls were identical with those of the Snake maid in the kiva during the dramatization about the Antelope altar at Walpi, and the two are supposed to be the same as the maids which are also represented by effigies on the Flute altars.

THE FLUTE BOYS

The Flute boys of the two Flute divisions were dressed alike, and were furnished with the same offerings. Each wore a feather in his hair and a white ceremonial kilt over his loins. The arms, body, and legs were naked, and each carried in his left hand a netted gourd with water from Toreva spring, and a wooden slat upon which was depicted an ear of corn to which a feather was tied. In his right hand he bore a small, black, painted stick about an inch long, with a yucca fiber loop, by which it was carried, slipped on the end of a stick not unlike those about the Antelope altars. His hair hung loosely down his back.

In all essential features the Flute boys were clothed and decorated in the same manner as the Snake youth in the kiva exercises of the

Walpi Antelope priests on the morning of the ninth day of the Snake
ceremonies, with the exception that the boy personating the Snake
youth carried a rattlesnake in one hand.   These Flute boys represent
the ancestral or cultus hero of the Flute society, and bear the same
relationship to the priests that the Snake youth (Tcüa tiyo) bears to
the Antelope-Snake fraternities.

STANDARD BEARERS

The small naked boys at the ends of the platoons carry the Flute
standards, which consist of long sticks to the ends of which skins of
mammals and feathers are tied, also a string to which red-stained
horsehair is attached.   The Flute standard corresponds to the Snake
standard (awata natci), consisting of bows and arrows with appended
objects, the most conspicuous of which is the string of red horsehair
borne by Wikyatiwa in the Snake dance.   This standard is set upright
on the roof of the room in which the Flute ceremonies are held, just
as the awata natcis are tied to the ladders of the Antelope and Snake
kivas, as shown in plates XLVII and LIV.

BEARER OF THE MOISTURE TABLET

One of the most conspicuous members of the first platoon was the
man who bore on his back a rectangular framework over which was
stretched a buckskin or cloth on which were painted, in bright colors,
a number of parallel lines dividing it into rectangular fields, with
borders of colored bands (plate LVIII).   On the upper edge of the tablet, which covered the entire back of its bearer, was a bunch of feathers, and along each of the other three sides was stretched a cord, from
which was suspended horsehair stained red.   On the sides of the tablet
were tied small round disks made of sections of gourd painted in colors,
possibly representing cornflowers.   A further description of one of
these tablets, with an illustration, has been given elsewhere.[1]

BEARER OF THE SUN EMBLEM

As previously stated, one of the Macileñya bore on his back a disk
representing the sun.   It was made of buckskin stretched over a hoop
which was strengthened by a framework of two sticks fastened at
right angles.   This disk, which was about a foot in diameter, was
surrounded by a plaited border made of corn husks, into which eagle
feathers and red-stained horsehair were inserted.   The sun shield was
attached to the back of the bearer by a cord over his shoulders.   The
body of the bearer was naked, save for a white ceremonial kilt with a
pendent foxskin, and he had a tuft of feathers on the crown of his
head.   He carried a flute upon which he played, and wore moccasins

---

[1] American Anthropologist, vol. V, number 3, pl. II.

MACILEÑYA SOCIETY OF MISHONGNOVI

M. Wright Gill.

PLATOONS OF FLUTE PRIESTS MARCHING FROM THE SPRING TO MISHONGNOVI

and anklets (see plate LX). The natural inference is that the man wearing the sun emblem in such a conspicuous way personated the sun.[1] It will be observed that one of the figurines on the Flute altar (figure 44) is represented with a flute to its mouth. The whole ceremony commemorates the advent of the Corn maids, called by the tutelary name of the society, the Flute maids, and just as the Sun is said to have drawn them to himself in ancient times, so now the descendants strive by the same method to tole the personators of the same maids into the pueblo.

THE WARRIOR

A man clothed as a warrior, wearing a buckskin on his back and carrying a quiver of arrows over his shoulder, followed the procession. He carried a bow in one hand and in the other a whizzer or bullroarer, which he twirled at intervals. The bundle which he bore is the clothing of certain of his fellow-priests which they have doffed and given him to carry to the mesa top.

Most of the Flute priests had corn plants in their belts, and a few of them carried cornstalks in their hands. This accords with one of the main objects of the Flute ceremony—the growth of corn, the Hopi national food.

MARCH FROM TOREVA TO THE PUEBLO

After the two platoons had formed on the edge of Toreva the chief of the Cakwaleñya sprinkled a line of sacred meal, across which he made three rain-cloud symbols and three parallel lines representing falling rain. The Blue Flute boy and girls who stood at his side on the line facing the mesa (plate LXIII) threw their offerings toward this figure—the former, the small stick of wood; the latter, the annulet made of twisted flag leaves. The chief picked up these objects and set them on the rain-cloud signs which he had drawn, and the three children, followed by the platoon of priests, advanced to the symbols, the men singing, accompanied by the flutists. The children bent over, and, inserting the ends of their sticks into the loops, raised the offerings and held them extended, as the whole platoon marched forward to another set of rain-cloud meal-symbols which the chief had made some distance from the first. The platoon of Macileñya followed, conducting the same performance as the Cakwaleñya. Thus along the trail from Toreva to the plaza the two platoons halted at intervals, repeating what has been described several times without variation, before they came to the pueblo. They halted three times and performed the same acts as they crossed the plaza until they stood before the

---

[1] The symbolism of the sun disk is illustrated in a memoir on Tusayan Katcinas in the Fifteenth Annual Report of the Bureau of Ethnology. The emblem borne on the back of the Flute man, above mentioned, is identical with that described in the article cited, save that the latter is surrounded by radiating eagle feathers.

kisi, in front of which they sang for some time. After the first platoon had sung their songs before the kisi, they handed the offerings borne by the boy and the girls to a man within it,[1] and retired to the chamber where their altar stood. The second platoon followed, doing the same, after which they likewise retired and the ceremony closed with purification and the dismantling of the altar.

During the march to the pueblo, and later, before the kisi, the priests sang Flute songs, accompanied by the flutists. These songs are among the most melodious in Hopi ceremonies, and are worthy of special study. The songs at the kisi were especially pleasing, and as each division stood before the cottonwood bower and sang, it made a fine exhibit of aboriginal worship.

FLUTE CEREMONY AT WALPI IN 1896

The exercises of the Flute priests at Walpi in 1896 began on August 12 and continued until August 21, when they closed with the public dance. The author was able to witness the rites celebrated on the 12th, 13th, and 14th of the month, finding in them considerable variation from those performed on the same relative days of 1892.[1]

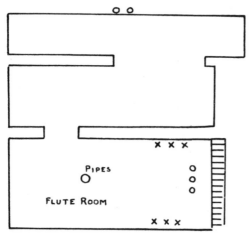

FIG. 45—Plan of Flute room at Walpi.

The significance of these variations is not known, but as material for an ultimate explanation it has been deemed advisable to record them.

The secret observances of the Walpi Flute ceremony occur in a large house on the north side of the pueblo, about opposite the passageway opening northward from the plaza in which the Snake dance is celebrated. This house (figure 45), the ancestral Flute chamber, has an open balcony in front and exemplifies an ancient form of architecture which has well-nigh been abandoned on the East mesa. It was the first home of the Flute clan after it moved to the mesa summit, the ancient home of the Snake clan being just above the so-called Snake rock, which rises from the south end of the main plaza. The two houses

---

[1] The Flute chief crawled into the kisi, and certain objects, as pahos, water gourds, and meal were passed in to him, but what occurred within was concealed from view. The small netted gourds of water which the boy and girls carried (plate LXIII) are the same as those used in the Snake dances.

[1] For an account of the Walpi Flute ceremony of 1892 see Journal of American Folk-Lore, vol. VII, number 26.

mentioned are separated by a court, and probably never adjoined. Other phratries, as the Patki and Honani, were formerly domiciled in houses separated from both the Snake and Flute dwellings, so that, originally, probably Walpi consisted of a number of small clusters of houses which, through later building, were in part consolidated into a compact pueblo.

There were present in the Flute chamber at about 10 oclock on the assembly day (August 12) the following priests: Tuᵣnoa, Flute chief; Hoñyi, speaker chief; Sikyabotima, courier, and another man. Later there came in Winuta, Hani, and one or two others who had been there earlier in the day. This was known from the fact that they did not make the customary offering of meal on their entrance. It is prescribed for a priest on entering a kiva for the first time to sprinkle with sacred meal any altar or fetishes which may be in place. An interesting altar had been erected in the Flute room, and as this altar is characteristic, a description of it will be desirable.

First Flute Altar

There were two Flute altars at Walpi, but neither of these pertained to the Drab Flute society, for this society is extinct at that pueblo. On the first day the Walpi Flute society erected their altar on a ridge of sand just in front of the stack of corn which filled one end of the Flute chamber. The altar (plate LXIV) is called the first Flute altar[1] to distinguish it from the second or main altar. As the songs of the first three days were sung by priests before this altar, it appears to be an important accessory in the Flute worship.

A low ridge of valley sand was made before the stacked corn at one end of the Flute chamber, and in this ridge, at regular intervals, were placed three tiponis, those of Tuᵣnoa, Winuta, and Hoñyi, respectively, beginning at the left. From Hoñyi's tiponi a line of meal extended across the floor toward the doorway, and over this line was stretched a string, to the extremity of which were fastened two feathers. The length of this string was measured from the finger tips of the outstretched arm to a point above the heart, and it was drawn through a handful of sacred meal before being laid in position. When each tiponi was ready to be set in place, the chief to whom it belonged first made six radiating lines on the sand ridge where it was to stand, and deposited half a handful of meal at their junction. On this the tiponi was placed.

On the floor in front of Tuᵣnoa's tiponi, there was a basket-tray containing sacred meal; a similar tray containing stringed feathers made

---

[1] Whether the other pueblos have a similar altar on the first day is unknown, since no one has fully studied the opening of the Flute ceremony in any other village. But probably it will be found that the societies in the other villages have an altar corresponding to this first Flute altar of Walpi.

by members of the society stood before Winuta's lodge, and the medicine bowl was on the floor near Hoñyi's tiponi.

Two bullroarers or whizzers lay on the floor by the medicine bowl and paho basket, and when returned to their position after being used, were always so placed that the strings were at the end toward the altar. All the priests accompanied their songs on small gourd rattles, but Tu'noa had a "moisture rattle," or paaya, which has already been figured and described.[1]

This altar is almost identical with that which is erected in the winter flute ceremony, and the same persons took part in almost identical rites about it.

The Second Flute Altar

The second or elaborate flute altar was erected on the fourth day. This the author was unable to see, being obliged to go to the Middle mesa on the morning of that day to witness parts of the Mishongnovi Flute ceremony.[2] All the parts of the altar were, however, examined as they lay on the floor, and drawings were made of several of them early in the morning of the day named.

The symbolism on the reredos of the Walpi flute altar was exceptional. The designs on the uprights were typical of flute altars, representing rain clouds and falling rain. An exceptional figure was a representation of the sun in the middle of the transverse part of the reredos. This figure does not occur in any of the other flute altars which have thus far been studied.

Elsewhere there have been figured the four slabs which stand about the upright stick on the roof of the Flute house at Shipaulovi on the final days of the ceremony.[3] As similar slabs, used for the same purpose at Walpi, have never been figured, for purposes of comparative study they are represented in the accompanying illustration (plate LXV). They are placed on the roof at the north, west, south, and east sides of the upright rod, or awati-natci, as is indicated by their respective colors—yellow, green, red, and white. During the morning of the fourth day they were all repainted.

Flute Songs

The exercises about the first flute altar began by a ceremonial smoke, during which Sikyabotima acted as pipe lighter, passing the pipe first to Tu'noa with the greeting "Inaa" ("My father"),[4] to which the Flute

---

[1] The Walpi Flute Observance, op. cit.

[2] It is next to impossible for one person to study thoroughly any great Tusayan ceremony during a single performance. Important rites are often being performed simultaneously in several rooms, while at the same time significant observances may take place in the plaza of the pueblo.

[3] Journal of American Ethnology and Archeology, vol. II.

[4] These two men are of about the same age, or, if there is any difference, the Flute chief is younger than Sikyabotima. The designation "My father" refers to society precedence, not to the family relationship. I have heard a young man of twenty ceremonially called "grandfather" by an old man of sixty or more. The terms "father," "son," "elder brother," "younger brother," etc., used in passing the pipe, are ceremonial, not family relationship terms.

LEÑYA (FLUTE) CHILDREN OF MISHONGNOVI

LEÑYA (FLUTE) CHILDREN OF MISHONGNOVI

chief responded with "Itii" ("My son"). He then lighted a second pipe and handed it to Hoñyi with the word "Itupko" ("My elder brother"), to which the response "Iviva" ("My younger brother") was given. After Hoñyi had smoked he returned his pipe to Sikyabotima, and the Flute chief did the same. Tuʳnoa, Hoñyi, Winuta, and Sikyaustiwa then prayed in sequence.

At the close of the prayers the songs began, the priests all keeping time by beating or shaking their rattles, and the Flute chief holding the paaya, or "moisture rattle," previously referred to. During the songs an old man cast pinches of meal to the cardinal points in sinistral sequence, and Winuta asperged medicine water toward the same directions by means of a feather.

When the songs were about half finished Sikyabotima took the whizzers or bullroarers from the floor before the altar and twirled them several times, after which he went into an adjoining room and repeated the same action. Hani accompanied the songs with a flute.[1] When the singing came to an end, prayers followed, and a ceremonial smoke closed the exercises.

Four chiefs were in the room on the opening day, and each of these made four nakwa kwoci or stringed feathers. No prayer-sticks were made on this day, nor on the next two days, a feature at variance with what occurred in the 1892 ceremony. The sixteen nakwakwoci were arranged in a basket-tray in four clusters indicating four cardinal directions, and were placed before the tiponis as shown in the illustration (plate LXIV). These were later offered to the gods of the four world-quarters. Pahos were said to have been made on the day on which the main altar was erected.

UNWRAPPING THE FLUTE TIPONI

The unwrapping of the flute tiponi took place on the second day at about 1.30 p. m., the time consumed being somewhat over an hour.

On entering the room the author found a number of Flute priests assembled, Winuta squatting on a white buckskin which had been spread over a white woolen blanket, beneath which was a red Navaho blanket of ordinary pattern. He wore a ceremonial kilt and had a feather tied to his scalp lock; otherwise he was naked. On the buckskin before him were spread, in regular rows, feathers and strings, with other appendages of the tiponi, the core of which he held in his hand. This core consisted of a wooden cup-shape object, in the cavity of which was inserted an ear of white corn with four black painted

---

[1] The so-called flute used in the flute ceremony is different from the instrument usually known by that name, in that the person using it does not blow across a hole in the side, but across a terminal opening, although producing the tone by the same mechanical principle. To the extremity of the instrument is attached a trumpet-like piece of gourd, which is sometimes painted in many colors. The operator fingers certain holes along the side of the flute while playing.

marks extending longitudinally (figure 46). The four quadrants of the cup were decorated on the exterior with symbols of corn and rain clouds, and on the base were two black lines crossing at right angles. There lay on the buckskin, at one side, another ear of corn, a quantity of cotton string, and many feathers which had been taken from the tiponi and rejected, for a new ear of corn was to replace the old, and new wrapping was to be added. The grains of corn from the old tiponi were later planted, and many of the feathers were placed in shrines.

In wrapping the tiponi the priest held the core in the left hand, and wound[1] the cotton string about it, inserting at times the feathers which protruded beyond the ear of corn. Suggestions were made in the course of the wrapping by several of those present, and many of the old feathers were replaced in the new bundle.

After the tiponi had been wrapped, and a string with attached shells added as a necklace, Winuta and Tu'noa, the young Flute chief, arose and stood on the blanket side by side, facing the east, Tu'noa being on the left. Both were naked save for a breechcloth, and Winuta held the tiponi in his right palm, grasping it midway of its length with his right hand. Winuta addressed a few words to Tu'noa, who responded "Antcai" ("It is well"). Hoñyi then took Winuta's place and spoke in the same strain to the Flute chief, who remained standing. The tiponi, which had been passed by Winuta to Hoñyi, was transferred by the latter to Sikyaustiwa, who followed the actions of the others by handing it to Hani, who made a fervent appeal and passed it to Tu'noa. After the Flute chief Tu'noa had received the palladium he carried it to the altar, and made with sacred meal, on the mound of sand where it formerly stood, six radiating lines, placing the tiponi at their junction. He then returned to that part of the room where the blankets had been spread on the floor, and smoked in silence for a long time.

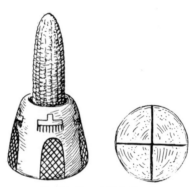

Fig. 46.—Core of Flute tiponi.

In a previous and fuller account of the renewal of the tiponi, in 1892, it was said to take place on the sixth day after the main altar had been erected. It is possible that this and other variations may in part be due to the death of the old Flute chief Cimo and the elevation of his younger successor Tu'noa.

[1]As he wound the tiponi he allowed the string to be drawn through his hand, which contained sacred meal. The winding was always toward the left, or in the direction called the sinistral ceremonial circuit.

The unwrapping of the tiponi has been witnessed in two Hopi ceremonies, the Flute and the Lalakonti. In these instances the contents
of the palladium varied, but in both either kernels of corn or other seeds
form essential parts. From chiefs of other societies it has been learned
that their tiponis likewise contained corn either in grains or on the ear.
Although from this information one is not justified in concluding that
all tiponis contain corn, it is probably true with one or two exceptions. The tiponi is called the "mother," and an ear of corn given to
a novice has the same name. There is nothing more precious to an
agricultural people than seed, and we may well imagine that during
the early Hopi migrations the danger of losing it may have led to
every precaution for its safety. Thus it may have happened that it
was wrapped in the tiponi and given to the chief to guard with all
care as a most precious heritage. In this manner it became a mere
symbol, and as such it persists to-day.

THE KISI

In no public ceremony of the Hopi is the cottonwood kisi introduced
except in the Snake and Flute rites, in both of which its construction is identical. This brush-house is doubtless a survival from very
ancient times, and is related with the history of the ceremony with
which it is connected. A line of meal is sometimes drawn around it.
It is stated by the Snake people that they were the original inhabitants of Walpi, and there is no doubt that the Bear, Snake, and Flute
clans formed the nucleus of the ancient pueblo of which Walpi is
the survivor. Equally emphatic is the claim of the Snake traditionists
that their ancestors came from the north, and other evidence tends to
substantiate the assertion. There is little difficulty in tracing a like-
ness between the kisis of the pueblos and the medicine-lodges of
nomadic tribes, but thus far there is nothing to prove the derivation of
one from another.

GENERAL REMARKS

Three elements appear to be prominent in the Flute observance,
viz, sun, rain, and corn worship, symbols of which are the most
prominent on the altars and their accessories. The same is true of
the Snake dance; but in both rites the cultus heroes and clan mothers
are special deities to which the supplications for rain and corn are
addressed. This is interpreted as a form of totemism in which the
ancestors of the clan take precedence. The Sun as the father of all
cultus heroes and the Earth as the mother of all gods, ancestral and
otherwise, necessarily form an important part of the worship, which
is traceable throughout both ceremonies.

Relation of Snake Society and Snake Clan

The Hopi ritual, or that part of it which pertains to communal worship, making up the yearly calendar, bears evidence of being composite, and we may suppose that it has become so for the same reasons that the social system of the Hopi is composite. It is composed of a collection of ceremonies which have come together, yet remain distinct. In the traditional account of the growth of Walpi, for instance, it is stated that families drifted to the site of the pueblo from different directions, and as they arrived certain sections of the village were assigned to them for their homes; these sections their descendants still occupy. By mutual consent each clan was allotted certain tracts of land in the plain for their farms, and these land holdings still remain in the clans. While the clans were living together, a community of interest developed and intermarriage broke down the limitation of sacerdotal societies to clans. Certain emergencies arose when clans were forced to act together. These influences resulted in an amalgamation of clans, and a new organization was effected. The clan languages were fused into a common speech, and a coalescence of the different arts and customs also occurred. The new organization retained much that was good in each of component clans.

The ritual developed along the same lines, but the religious sentiment being more conservative, the clan units have remained more apparent in the rites than elsewhere. When each new family joined the already established villagers, it brought its own mythology and ritual clustering about a special cultus hero and clan mother, or tutelary ancestral couple and, after the union with other clans continued to practice its own clan rites. The germ of that clan ancients worship was evidently ancestor worship. The Hopi ritual is thus a composite of several distinctive clan units.

The Snake dance and the Flute observance are two of these units—one the clan worship of the Snake clans, the other that of the Flute clans. Moreover, since these two clans were among the first to unite and form the nucleus of Walpi, their clan rites must necessarily have been practiced side by side for a longer time than those of most other clans. Hence we should expect to find mutual reaction and many pronounced similarities, which account for the ritualistic resemblances noted, and also afford a verification of the legend of the antiquity of the Snake and Flute ceremonies at Walpi; but there is nothing to show that they are older than the others, although good evidence exists that they have been observed at Walpi for a longer time than any other forms of clan worship. It would be interesting to know the sources and characteristics of the subsequent increments to the Walpi ritual, but the Snake and Flute clan rites are preeminently attractive to the ethnologist.

A correct determination of the relationship between the clan and the sacerdotal society is important if we would gain a clear idea of the character and history of the Hopi ritual. There is no doubt that at present the sacerdotal society includes in its numbers members of several clans, and is not confined to any particular one. Consequently those who conclude that the two organizations are distinct at the present time are justified in that conclusion; but that does not prove that they always were distinct. Evidently in ancient times, when all the inhabitants of Walpi belonged to the Snake clans, the Snake priesthood was limited to that clan, and if the inhabitants of that ancestral pueblo celebrated the Snake dance it was, strictly speaking, a family affair. After the Flute, the Rain-cloud, Badger, and other groups of clans joined the Snake village, men from these clans became members of the Snake priesthood, giving the present composite personnel which intermarriage made inevitable. The retention of the Snake chieftaincy in the Snake clan in a matriarchal line of descent is one of the many survivals of the former limitation of the Snake priesthood to the Snake clans. A custom in passing the pipe in the ceremonial smoking is another survival. The terms "father," "grandfather," "son," "brother," "elder brother," "younger brother," which are exchanged at that time do not now indicate clan relationship, as hitherto explained, but are survivals of a time when they did. A youth of 18 may be called "grandfather" by a man of 60, and when Hahawe passes the pipe to Wiki and calls him "my elder brother," and Wiki responds "my younger brother," neither of these priests means that the other is his clan relative—it is the relationship of the sacerdotal standing of one to the other that is indicated. The terms are survivals of a time when they meant blood kinship, for when the ceremony was limited to the clan, Wiki, the chief, was "elder brother," or "father," or "grandfather," to the man who thus addressed him. The formal address survives, although the man using it may now belong to a different clan from that of the chief.

RELATION OF THE FLUTE SOCIETY AND FLUTE CLAN

In the same way that the Snake and Antelope fraternities are or were directly related to, and were introduced into Walpi by, the Snake and Horn clans, so the Flute societies originated with the Flute clans and were added by them to the participants in the Hopi ritual when they joined preexisting families. Before the Flute clans came to Walpi, bringing their cultus, they had amalgamated with the Horn clans, which had earlier lived with the Snake clans at a place called Tokonabi. Naturally a result of this consolidation was a modification of the Flute ceremony, and the result of this influence was the likenesses between

19 ETH, PT 2——29

portions of the Snake dance and the Flute ceremony due to Horn clans common to the Horn-Snake and the Horn-Flute groups of clans.

There is good reason to believe that the Flute clans, and hence the Flute societies, came to Tusayan from the south, whereas the Horn and Snake clans came from the north, or Tokonabi.

Ophiolatry in the Snake Dance

The Snake dance is a celebration or worship of the cultus hero and clan mother (Tcüamana) of the Snake clan, but not of the Great Plumed Snake (Palülükoñ), which the legends say was introduced by the Patki clans from the south. These legends are supported by the fact that the effigies of the Plumed Snake are used in the Soyaluña and Palülükoñti ceremonies by the Patki and other southern clans, and not by the Snake society in its worship. No reference to Palülükoñ occurs in the legend of the Snake clans, but a figure of it is painted on the kilts of the Snake priests. These facts have led to the belief that the worship of a Great Snake was foreign to the ritual of Walpi when its population was composed only of Snake, Horn, and Flute clans; that it came to Walpi after the Snake clan was established in that pueblo, and hence presumably after the Snake dance had been introduced. The presence of reptiles in the Snake ceremony is generally supposed to show that this rite is a form of snake worship. It is rather a worship of the ancestors of the Snake clans, which are anthropo-zoömorphic beings, called the Snake youth and the Snake maid; but neither of these represent the Great Snake, nor has their worship anything to do with that of this personage, who was introduced into Hopi mythology and ritual by the Rain-cloud clans. As personated in the Antelope kiva at Walpi, these ancestral beings have no reptilian characteristics, and the snakes which are introduced in the ceremonies are not worshiped, but are regarded as the "elder brothers" of the priests. It is not supposed that these reptiles have any more power to send rain than the "elder brothers" or shades of deceased members of any other society. They are intercessors between man and the rain gods, and if the proper ceremonies with them are performed in prescribed sequence and in traditional ways, the rains must come because they came in the ancient times in the house of the Snake maid. The idea of magic permeates the whole ceremony, which is not an appeal to a great Snake deity to grant any definite request, but a compulsion of the rain and growth supernaturals to perform their functions, which is brought about by the use of proper charms.

The Hopi conception of the rain gods involves no limitation of these supernaturals to definite numbers. There is no suggestion of a single anthropomorphic being which sends the rain, but Rain-cloud spirits are associated with the six cardinal points, and are regarded as ancestral beings.

M. Wright Gill

FLUTE CHILDREN OF MISHONGNOVI THROWING OFFERINGS ON RAIN-CLOUD SYMBOLS

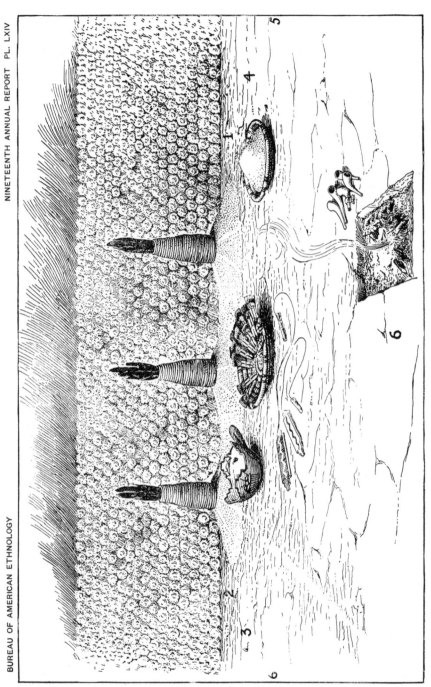

FIRST FLUTE ALTAR AT WALPI

Relative Place of the Snake Dance in Primitive Worship

The present purpose of the Snake ceremony, which in many publications has been confounded with its original aim, is primarily, as has been elsewhere shown, to bring rain and thus to promote the growth of corn; in fact this desire, due to present environment, dominates all the rites of the Hopi ritual. It is believed, however, that this is not original meaning—back of it is a psychic element which the Hopi share with other primitive people whose myths and ritual have not been modified by an arid climate and an agricultural life. We must look more deeply into the subject in order to bring the Snake dance into harmony with the elements of religion in a more primitive mind.

It has been shown that in the Snake ceremony there is no worship of the Great Serpent, and the Snake priests scout the idea that this great deity belonged to their clan worship. In support of their claims it may be mentioned that Palülükoñ is not represented on their altars. The psychic element of religion in the Snake dance is totemic ancestor worship, which is fundamental in the whole Hopi ritual. The reptile is a society totem, the lineal survivor of a clan totem, and the totem ancestor, called the Snake maid, is, generally, like totemic ideas, an anthropo-zoömorphic conception. Members of the society claim immunity from the bite of the snake because it is their totem, and the idea of possession of the shade or "breath-body" of the dead by the snake totem is in accord with universal totemic conceptions.

The Snake dance is simply a form of clan totemism having special modifications, due to environment, to fit the needs of the Hopi. It is a highly modified form of ancestor worship in which the Sun and the Earth, as parents of all, are worshiped, but in which the cultus hero and the ancestors of the clan are the special divinized personages represented in secret rites.

Interpretation of Snake and Flute Rites

The main object of the majority of Hopi ceremonials is the production of rain and the growth of corn. The reason for individual rites must be sought in certain universal principles of religion common to all men. There are three primal elements which permeate all Hopi ceremonies—the gods, the worshiper, and the needs of the latter, or what he wishes to obtain from the former. Ceremony is largely, if not wholly, made up of the methods adopted by the worshiper, man, to influence the gods to grant his wishes, and is directly the outgrowth of prayer, which is a reflection of desire or want, which in turn is the outgrowth of climatic influences. Agriculturists desire rain and crops. and they pray to the gods especially for these things. There are

certain ways of expressing their prayers, which are known as ceremonies—the nature of the prayer being intimately connected with the
conception of the nature of the gods and the understanding of the
wants of the worshiper by himself.

There are several kinds of prayer, and there is varying development
in the accompanying symbolism. The verbal prayer is one type,
which is universal. In this the worshiper simply asks the gods in
his own langüage for what he wants. This form of prayer originated
at a time when the gods were regarded as zoömorphic and anthropomorphic, and implies a god who speaks and who hears the desires of
his worshiper. In the long process of evolution, however, the verbal
prayer became something more than a simple request—the words came
to have symbolic meanings and as such were media of communion with
gods. They became expressions of religious feeling, but were not
necessary to the existence of that feeling. Many worshipers were
thus led to drop them and to preserve the feeling in silent prayers;
others, reverencing the ancient forms, retained the words as symbolic
aids. In the growth of religion it was early recognized that the gods
had their own language and that possibly they were unable to understand that of men; hence, as has been shown by Powell, there arose
and developed a religious gesture language, or an expression of prayer
by dramatization. The worshiper in this type of prayer, which may
be called dramatic prayer, showed the gods through action what he
desired. He combined it with verbal prayer, with symbolic prayer,
but the dramatic element was always most striking. Ceremony, in
the main, but not wholly, is highly developed dramatic prayer, and the
object of dramatic prayer is to show by acting what the worshiper
desires.

In order to appeal to the gods in this gesture language, symbolism
is largely employed in the paraphernalia used in worship. Let us
apply this to the altars. The prayers of agriculturists in an arid
environment are necessarily for rain and the growth of crops—in the
case of the Hopi, of maize, their national food—and certainly no one,
god or human, could look upon a Hopi altar without seeing symbols
of these two things—rain clouds, falling rain, lightning, and corn and
other seeds. On the altar are placed either the symbols of what is
wanted or the objects themselves. To be sure, there are other objects,
but these are supplementary, and vary, but rain symbols and corn
symbols are universal.

Not only are the desired objects thus symbolically represented as
silent prayers to convey the desire to the gods, but personations of
ancestral gods, either in the form of idols or representations by human
beings, are found on the same altars. These are not the gods—they
are only symbols—temporary residences, if you wish, of the gods.
Here we have a still more realistic evolution of the dramatic prayer.

A. ROEN & CO. LITHOCAUSTIC, BALTIMORE

CAKWALEÑYA ALTAR SLABS AT WALPI

"A SNAKE PRIEST", HOPI, ARIZONA, 1900, PHOTO BY EDWARD S. CURTIS, COURTESY OF THE MUSEUM OF NEW MEXICO, NEG. NO. 173451

The priest prays to this representation of the god by scattering meal upon it, and the god has but to look about him on the altar to know what is wanted. Observe how the pantomime of imitating falling rain is performed in this way. The priest dips his aspergill in the medicine and asperges in turn to the six cardinal points in representation of falling rain, and this is symbolic of what the priest wishes the gods of the six directions to do.

The priest at another time asperges on a sand-picture symbol of a rain-cloud for the same reason—he shows what he wishes the Rain gods to do, viz, to sprinkle the earth with rain.

Again, the priest pours water into his medicine bowl from six directions to show the gods that he desires them to send rain from the six directions of the known world. He blows an immense cloud of smoke on the altar because he wishes clouds to appear. The act has the same significance—it is a prayer for the rain-cloud which the Rain gods may understand. For this purpose also the priest sounds his whizzer—to imitate the thunder which accompanies the rain.

For this same purpose also the figures of aquatic animals—the tadpole and the frog—which supposedly bring the rain, are displayed because they are silent prayers for rain. Hence, also, the Antelope priests wear rain-cloud symbols on their kilts and zigzag lightning marks on their bodies and limbs.

RELEASING THE SNAKES, SNAKE DANCE, HOPI ARIZONA, CA 1911, PHOTO BY
H.F. ROBINSON, COURTESY OF THE MUSEUM OF NEW MEXICO, NEG. NO. 37044